# Beyond Bottles Baths & Bed

The Complete Guide to Raising Happy Emotionally Connected Kids

Cherie King

First published by Ultimate World Publishing 2024
Copyright © 2024 Cherie King

ISBN

Paperback: 978-1-923123-29-8
Ebook: 978-1-923123-30-4

Cherie King has asserted her rights under the Copyright, Designs and Patents Act 1988 to be identified as the author of this work. The information in this book is based on the author's experiences and opinions. The publisher specifically disclaims responsibility for any adverse consequences which may result from use of the information contained herein. Permission to use information has been sought by the author. Any breaches will be rectified in further editions of the book.

All rights reserved. No part of this publication may be reproduced, stored in or introduced into a retrieval system, or transmitted in any form, or by any means (electronic, mechanical, photocopying, recording or otherwise) without the prior written permission of the author. Any person who does any unauthorised act in relation to this publication may be liable to criminal prosecution and civil claims for damages. Enquiries should be made through the publisher.

**Cover design:** Ultimate World Publishing
**Layout and typesetting:** Ultimate World Publishing
**Editor:** Vanessa McKay
**Cover Image Copyright:** Kraphix-Shutterstock.com

Ultimate World Publishing
Diamond Creek,
Victoria Australia 3089
www.writeabook.com.au

# Dedication

To my two amazing children, Jake and Samara and my precious grandson, Hudson, thank you for being my source of inspiration.

*Children are the rainbow of Life. Grandchildren are the Pot of Gold*

To my Dad - The man who taught me to dream and supported me in every step, your love is one of my greatest treasures.

# Testimonials

Cherie King is a genius! Her insight into this topic, coupled with a wealth of experience gained over the many years of teaching is evident in this book. You are compelled to keep turning the pages, and when you do, somehow there's a feeling of reassurance that leaps out at you and says "hey, I think I've done ok here!" A must read for all parents and caregivers from toddlers to teens, Beyond Bottles, Baths and Bed will resonate with so many, as it did for me.
**Nina Woulfe- Director Trio Support**

If you can relate to the 'role of parenting' being described as a "roller-coaster ride", then this book is for you. Cherie has gifted us an easy to read, practical, thought provoking and realistic guide to "growing emotionally happy" and resilient kids.

Not everyone has the passion or the ability to translate into print, lifelong learning experiences, skills, knowledge and authentic practices aimed at improving the happiness and security of kids, but, Cherie does. As a dynamic, compassionate and committed educator, a loving mother, a loyal and respected friend to many, Cherie is well placed to do this.

This book is one that you will read over and over again.

Not only will it guide you in supporting your child and grandchildren, it will allow you to nurture and understand how you relate and care for your own relationships and friendships.

**Wendy Graham – Former Primary School Principal**

Cherie brought a breath of fresh air to my life with her vibrant, considerate & caring personality. It is a challenge to summarise the skills Cherie has displayed within her family, the community & around her friends. Cherie is a REAL person with REAL abilities to transfer her knowledge to all seeking the ongoing connection with their children. Her life experiences with thousands of children, through her many years of teaching, her own two children & now grandchild are priceless & endless. Cherie has always had the eyes to see and the ears to hear.

My feeling is that Cherie had a strong urge to fly, and now has somewhere to fly to – that is….your hearts and what is precious to you. You are completely safe in her competent & passionate hands while reading this book.

**Kearen Griffiths – Friend**

This book comes to you from the heart and mind of my good friend Cherie King. From her many years of being a loving mother, educator and new grandmother, she has deep respect for children and their families. Providing them with love and knowledge to support their journey, that we as parents, aunts, uncles and grandparents crave as we negotiate our way through life. Being a mother of 3 beautiful girls, all with 2 children, each of their own and have worked in the early childhood industry for 24 years, I

*Testimonials*

feel that the edition of a copy of Beyond Bottles, Baths and Bed to your home library will be beneficial to the whole family to read and grow with.

**Gay Moore – Friend and Childcare Teacher**

Featuring tangible strategies for parents, Beyond Bottles, Baths and Bed provides an advice filled guide to navigating the experience of parenting.

Built on personal experience and a wealth of knowledge from many years in education, it celebrates, inspires and supports parents to navigate life's tricky parenting moments.

This easy read will create calm and provide reassurance during the adventures of raising happy emotionally connected kids.

**Andrew Kinniburgh – Behaviour Specialist Advisor NSW Dept Education**

Having known Cherie, personally and professionally for many years, there is no one more qualified to give advice on raising happy emotionally connected children. This book breaks down the biggest worries for new parents. In a world where parenting is heavily scrutinised, Cherie's simple words "show up for your kids" puts it all into perspective. Beyond Bottles, Bath and Bed is a must read for all new parents!

**Linda King – Friend and Primary School Senior Administration Manager**

Cherie King's "down to earth" style and over 30 years of professional wisdom make the insights in this book a MUST for new parents who are looking to not just "get their kids to behave" but to help them grow into the gorgeous humans they are meant to be.

Parenting is bloody hard, we want what's best for our kids and yes, life CAN get in the way. This book is a reminder, as well as a practical guide, to creating a connection with our kids that not only helps in those challenging behavioural moments, but also allows us to relate to them and understand their own unique language. It's a window into a new paradigm for parenting.
**Kirsty Verity CEO and Founder,
Kirsty Verity Consulting**


Cherie's book helps us to look beyond our imperfections, allow ourselves grace on this parenting journey and to listen to our instincts. It's about a journey of forgiveness and growth and the importance of repairing those, sometimes all too often, ruptures with our children without holding onto the guilt of what could have been different. Cherie's book has come at a time where childhood and adolescent mental illness is at all time high.

This book serves as a guide for any parent or caregiver of children to strengthen their attachment and understanding of their child to foster positive wellbeing and developmental outcomes into adulthood. Throw "that" baby book out and allow yourself the opportunity to grow and learn with Beyond Bottles, Baths and Bed!
**Kathryn Stephens – Child Protection Practice Leader**

# Contents

| | |
|---|---|
| Introduction | 1 |
| Chapter 1: Parenting: Job or Journey? | 3 |
| Chapter 2: Nurturing Potential: Brain Development | 17 |
| Chapter 3: Growing Your Child's Happy Emotional World: The Key Ingredient | 31 |
| Chapter 4: Showing Up: What Impacts our Ability? | 45 |
| Chapter 5: Regulation: The Key to Taming Big Emotions | 57 |
| Chapter 6: Happiness Unleashed: The Hidden Power of Emotional Intelligence | 75 |
| Chapter 7: Caring for the Caretaker: Embracing Looking After You | 89 |
| Chapter 8: One-of-a-Kind: Recognising the Beauty of Our Uniqueness | 105 |
| Chapter 9: The Inner Compass: Mastering The 8th Sense - Interoception | 117 |
| Chapter 10: Creating Moments of Magic: Embracing The Power of Play | 131 |
| Chapter 11: Pandemic Fallout: How to Support Through Challenging Times | 145 |
| Chapter 12: Connect and Play to Thrive: You've Got This! | 161 |
| Acknowledgments | 171 |
| About the Author | 173 |
| References | 175 |
| Bibliography | 181 |
| Kick Start or Supercharge Your Connection Journey | 185 |

# Introduction

"At the moment I know what he needs from me when he's upset, he either needs a feed, a nappy change or a sleep, but I just don't know what to expect and I worry I won't know what to do for Hudy if he's upset when he is a bit older, how will I know what he needs from me?"

These were the words of my beautiful daughter, Samara, who is a new mum and doing an amazing job of first-time parenting. Her words resonated deeply with me, as I felt that way when I had her older brother and was navigating the world of parenting for the first time. I remember so clearly the roller coaster ride of parenting in the early days, flying by the seat of my pants and hoping for the best! As luck would have it, somehow my husband and I fluked it and raised two amazing humans who we continue to be incredibly proud of.

Samara's words stayed with me, and it had me not only reflecting on my parenting journey but also on my teaching career, having worked with thousands and thousands of children over the years. What had I learnt about kids? And what was it that made the difference to children in the early days of their precious little lives? The answer was incredibly simple - the difference is the parent or carer. It is not about geography, status, or cultural background, quite simply, it is about a caring, attentive adult that consistently shows up for the child and does their best. This creates secure attachment.

This was particularly highlighted for me when I reflected on the many children and young people I have worked with that have experienced trauma in their lives. Through many conversations and interaction with little people who were displaying complex and challenging behaviours, often the trigger or activation for an escalation in behaviour was the child's perceived threat to their safety. Which when further unpacked almost always led back to the child's early life experiences and what's incredible about this is some of those experiences could have been in utero.

So this book was born! But to be blatantly clear this is not a 'how to parent perfectly' manual, (because as we all know, there is no such thing as perfect parenting) in fact the goal for the words and pages within this book is to reassure you that you are not alone. I can guarantee you that every single parent around the globe will have, at some point in their parenting journey, thought, *what the hell do I do here?* Or have felt they have made a parenting misstep or have lost it with their child – it is all very normal. The information contained within is simple and offers easy ways to connect with your kids in the early years, to build secure attachment and set them up for life long positive outcomes, through 'good enough' parenting. Because the reality is, we will all make mistakes in our parenting journey, but there is opportunity to repair the ruptures, through continually showing up for our kids, no matter what. And by showing up we learn about what our kids need from us in moments of overwhelm and dysregulation, and when they know we see them for who they are, they feel valued, seen, safe and secure - the recipe for raising happy emotionally connected kids.

# Chapter 1

# Parenting: Job or Journey?

*"Stop fearing the mess and the chaos of the moment and embrace a long view of parenting. Believing that parenting is a marathon and not a sprint encourages us to keep going and not to get stuck on the hard days or even the hard years."*
*Dr Jeffrey & Amy Olrcik (2020)*

Every single one of us has our very own personal stories, perceptions and understandings about parenting. Heck, we could all call ourselves parenting experts (even though I think there is no such thing) as we have all been parented and have experienced parenting, so that gives us some sort of lived experienced qualification, right? Well yes and no, because I guess we understand what parenting looks, feels and sounds like through our own experience, but do we really know what's happening behind the scenes (inside the brain and body) for humans as we move through the journey of growing, changing and getting older? I know I didn't have a clue about brain development, secure attachment and the likes when I was parenting my kids. I think I was like most of the population of new parents, I just basically winged it and hoped for the best.

There is a societal assumption that just because we have the ability to procreate, we can parent and parent well. The reality is there is a huge variation in understanding and perception about what constitutes 'good' parenting, or parenting that supports our kids to develop into well balanced humans, who lead happy and fulfilling lives. This is to be expected because as humans we are all unique and have had a multitude of individual experiences that have been influenced by many things including, cultural backgrounds, religion, socioeconomic background, education, environment and opportunity.

The one thing I know from working as a teacher and leader of schools, is that every parent wants the very best for their child regardless of what's happening right in that moment, be it challenging, joyful, annoying or outright crazy!

All the parents I have met, have wanted what they perceive to be the best for their child. I've held on to this premise tightly for many years, and it was especially helpful when I had to meet with parents of kids who I had to have tough conversations with, about their child's behaviour.

One particular story that stays with me is the time I had a parent storm into my office, following a phone conversation only an hour earlier, wanting to tear my throat out because I was about to suspend their year five child for verbally abusing and spitting at a teacher.

It took all my reserves to remain calm whilst the parent yelled and slammed their fist on the table, demanding that I revoke the suspension. As the 'discussion' continued, it became apparent that the parent did not want their child being perceived as the 'naughty kid' or missing out on learning, during the period they would be out of school. What the parent wanted for their child was to be accepted for who they are (as we all do for our kids) and liked by kids and teachers. Now none of what this parent wanted for their child was unreasonable. In fact, it was beautiful, it was just the delivery of their message wasn't quite as beautiful.

And just so you know, the parent did eventually calm down and my throat remained intact, but I did not revoke the suspension, however I reduced the number of days and worked with the parent, child and teacher to repair the relationship rupture. I used to see that parent around town every so often and they would smile and wave and I would do the same. After all, our kids can make us do crazy things sometimes, just because we love them so deeply and want the best for them.

What's all this got to do with the title of this chapter - Parenting - Job or Journey?

Well, as I continued my research into neuroscience and throughout my many years of teaching, I noticed a subtle change in the language and the conversations I was having about parenting and different parenting styles. I'd like to take you on a little history trip to add some context and understanding of where we have been and where the science and research indicate we are headed.

As we progress, I am sure there will be elements of the journey that feel familiar to you, as we cut across generations of understanding and experiences in parenting. The information provided offers a broad overview of parenting across eras as countless variations exist, shaped by individual experiences, parental expectations, and cultural influences.

## *1960s -1970s*

Let's start way back in the 1960s, when some critical research was undertaken by psychologist Diana Baumrind, where she identified three different parenting styles; authoritative, authoritarian and permissive. Traditional parenting in the good old days had many facets of what is now commonly known as an authoritarian style. The authoritarian style of parenting was characterised by high demands and expectations from parents, but with a low responsiveness from them. What that means is the parenting style was marked by a strong emphasis on control, discipline, and high expectations, but it lacked warmth and connection. The role of parenting was mostly viewed as a job; a responsibility that requires time, effort and dedication.

It was the era of children who should be seen and not heard and showing them too much affection or love could potentially spoil them, leading to a child who would not be able to cope out in the big wide world. That was the general assumption anyway. I have to admit, when I read this research, my mind boggled as I grappled with the thought of not being playful or affectionate with my own kids.

But to be fair, the world was very different back then, and the research was only just beginning to be shared and was most likely only accessed through libraries and hardcover books for the majority of the population. There was no worldwide web back in the 60s! And if I may say so, it would be a very big assumption to think all the parenting research and journal articles of that time would have had a borrowing waitlist. So, in essence, parents just got on with it and parented in a way they thought was best (based on their own experiences). During the 60s and 70s having well-mannered kids that respond appropriately on cue, didn't fight, swear, answer back or misbehave was the measure of being a successful parent. It was during this period also that the use of punitive type responses such as smacking was much more prevalent, with the understanding being, if the child misbehaved and they received a good 'belting', they would be less likely to repeat the same action or engage in similar misbehaviour.

Whether it was right or wrong, that was the general societal perception or understanding of what good parenting looked like.

It makes me feel for those children, we all know them, those that are wild and free. I wonder what that did to their spirit and growth as a unique individual, as they attempted to fit into the rigid expectations of what being a child was meant to look and feel like, as directed by their parents.

## *1980s- 1990s*

The 1980s and 1990s were a very transformative period in parenting, with societal shifts and technological advancements having significant influence on the way parents approached raising their children. It was during the very early part of the 1980s that we were introduced to the term 'Helicopter Parenting'. I found this concept amusing at first, but as I learned more about the term and seeing it when interacting with the many parents whose children I taught, it became less amusing and more interesting to me.

The emergence of the phenomenon known as helicopter parenting was driven by the desire of some parents who were intent on protecting their children from harm at all costs by adopting a more hands-on, sometimes overprotective approach. This era also saw parents being increasingly involved in their child's activities, including schoolwork, extracurricular interests, and their social lives. A rise in organised playdates, closely monitored outings, and a degree of hyper-vigilance also marked this period.

My first experience of a helicopter parent was during the early years of my teaching career. The parent of Ruby, (not her actual name) a year 3 student, was so invested in the safety of her child that she would drop her at the classroom door in the morning and then return for morning tea and lunch breaks to monitor Ruby's s interactions and games, whilst she was not under my direct supervision. Whilst I understood and acknowledged Ruby's Mum's anxiety about her child's safety, it meant that Ruby could not independently explore friendships and her environment, without some level of input from her parent., This meant Ruby was somewhat dependent on the external validation from her Mum, rather than trusting and making her own decisions about who she played with and what she played. Ruby's mum eventually reduced the amount of time she was in the playground, but it did take nearly a whole term and lots of support from myself and other school staff to help her to feel comfortable to leave Ruby for the day

Perpetuating the helicopter parenting style was the significant influence of many things, including television and technology. It was during this period there was widespread availability of televisions and access to and use of personal computers. And the biggest influence of all was the introduction of a tool called the World Wide Web, aka the internet, and boy did that lead to a seismic shift in people's lives! We were no longer confined to our local space but we could access the world from our living room, a concept that was both scary and completely new for parents.

These innovations deeply influenced the way parenting was approached, as television became more and more a central form of entertainment and information for families, leading to debates about screen time and its potential effects on children's development. Along with television the introduction of personal computers bought both educational opportunities and concerns about children spending too much time on screens.

The 1980s and 1990s also saw a surge in parenting literature and resources. Books like "The Baby Book" by Dr. William Sears and Martha Sears, and "Parenting with Love and Logic" by Foster Cline and Jim Fay were popular, along with parenting magazines and television talk shows. Parents had access to a plethora of tips and hints about everything—from toddler taming to navigating adolescents. TV shows, such as Oprah and Dr. Phil, provided a platform for discussing parenting and this gave experts and parents a chance to chat about different ways to raise kids.

Whilst parenting in the era of the helicopter parent was characterised by a mix of cautiousness and enthusiasm, it also laid the groundwork for many trends that would continue to evolve in the 21st century, which ultimately shaped the way parents, parent today.

It was during the late 1990s that I became a parent for the first time and naively thought I knew all there was to know about being a parent, because hey, I had almost five years of working with kids under my belt, but little did I know, I was about to find out that I actually didn't have a bloody clue!

## *2000 and Beyond*

Enter where we are today, a time where the traditional family model of the 20th century, characterised by a father as the breadwinner, a mother managing the household and multiple children, has undergone transformations. Over the years, there has been an increase in blended and solo parent households, families have become smaller and individuals are opting to become parents later in life or deciding not to have kids at all.

We are in a time where research has ramped up and conversations about parenting have become even more mainstream, with Mums and Dads all over the world getting together for organised play group activities or leveraging the power of the internet to share and consume all things parenting. The internet has brought immediate answers, relief and confidence, but also pressure, as social media has become a platform for sharing life as a parent, but interestingly enough, mostly just the good stuff, not so much of the real, hard core, screamy moments of parenting. Which I can almost understand as nobody wants to see my kid on the ground thrashing around, because I cut their sandwich into squares, not triangles.

*Parenting: Job or Journey?*

We are in an era filled with terms like; 'phubbing'(also known as, technoference) which describes how technology is interrupting communication between parents and children and there is also 'sharenting'; where parents overshare information about their children on social media. Who doesn't love a bit of neologism? What is neologism you may ask? It's a term, word, or phrase that has emerged fairly recently or is unique and has gained popularity or recognition within society, gradually integrating itself into the common language used by the general population.

It is also a time of, apart from the more traditional parenting methods, many alternative approaches are becoming more mainstream. Some you may have heard of already, but others may be completely new to you, as they were to me, when I started writing this book.

Just for interest's sake, the list below summarises some current parenting styles as noted in the *OECDiLibrary Chapter 4: Educating 21st Century Children: Emotional Wellbeing in the Digital Age* research paper.

- Authoritarian
- Authoritative
- Permissive
- Uninvolved/ Neglectful
- Attachment/ Intuitive/Natural
- Free- range
- Lawn mower/Snow plough (my personal favourite)
- Narcissistic/ Accessory
- Positive

If you are interested in exploring some of these parenting styles the website can be found in the references section at the back of the book.

It also needs to be noted that many of these approaches are advocated as novel ways of parenting aimed at increasing children's success in education (think tiger parenting), professional settings, and life in general. It is interesting to note, many claims about the potential advantages of modern parenting approaches lack solid evidence from research, and in certain instances, these claims haven't been investigated thoroughly at all.

But thankfully, it is also a time of an amazing amount of research and very clever scientists, who are digging deeper into what our kids need from us, over and above the basics, such as food, a clean bum and sleep.

Much of the current science and research is pointing us towards the need to be aware of and focus our energies on meeting the hard wired needs of our kids, and that is the need for connection and belonging. Sounds pretty straight forward right? Well, yes it does, but what does it actually mean? What does it look like and feel like for us and our kids? I am going to go out on a limb here and suggest that most of us (including me at the start of my journey) could not easily articulate how I could support and build my child's, sense of connection to me, their Dad or other significant people in their lives. As for supporting their sense of belonging, I just assumed that would be a byproduct of being part of our amazing little family. That was until I started reading and listening to Dr Brene Brown, when she shared an anecdote in her book, *Daring Greatly,* about the research she did in a high school, where she asked some eighth graders to come up with the difference between *fitting in* and *belonging* and what she learned was nothing short of mind blowing for her and it absolutely stopped me in my tracks too.

Here's an example of what some students said:

> *"Belonging is being somewhere you want to be, and they want you."*

> *"Fitting in is being somewhere where you really want to be, but they don't care one way or the other."*

> *"Belonging is being accepted for you. Fitting in is being accepted for being like everyone else."*

> *"I get to be me if I belong. I have to be like you to fit in."*

Incredible wisdom from some very astute 15 year olds! But what you are about to read next, in my opinion is one of the most powerful statements from that focus group research, where one student said:

> *"Not belonging at school is really hard. But it's nothing compared to what it feels like when you don't belong at home."*

If that doesn't get you fair and square in the feels, I'd be very surprised. When Dr Brown dug a little further and asked students what they thought that meant, they provided the following responses:

> *"Not living up to your parent's expectations."*

*"Not being as cool or as popular as your parents want you to be."*

*"Not being as smart as your parents."*

*"Not being good at the same things your parents were good at."*

*"Your parents being embarrassed because you don't have enough friends or not an athlete or cheerleader."*

*"Your parents not liking who you are or what you like to do."*

*"When you parents don't pay attention to your life."* [1]

All very big statements that run deep for the young people who may be feeling that way.

Which got me thinking about this whole parenting gig - what is it that our kids need from us to have a connection and a deep sense of belonging that feeds their identity and sense of self-worth? After years of devouring research articles, journals and leaning on my many years of teaching and leadership experience, each path led me to the conclusion that parenting for connection and emotional wellbeing is not about asking, "What do I do?" when things are tough but asking, "How shall I be with my child?".

These are two questions that can produce two very different responses. As we talk more in future chapters, the essence of being with your child will become clearer and may be something you will consider when things turn to poo. The beauty of being with your child is that when we get it wrong, and we will, because we are human, there is an opportunity to repair and grow the relationship. These are the moments, amongst others, that will stay with your child, build connection and reassure them they belong, as you see them and value them for who they are.

And in more recent times there has been a paradigm shift in the way behavior is managed, with a move towards understanding what our children's behavior is communicating to us, rather than viewing challenging behaviour as just being plain naughty; to seeing challenging behavior as a symptom not a problem.

And the best news about all of this is; there is no such thing as perfect parenting, good enough parenting is good enough and the even better news is that it is never too late!! Trust me, I am still the goddess of good enough parenting with our two adult children, but they know I am doing my best with what I know. So, I don't want anyone reading this to think that they may have made a mess of things, because, well, you haven't. You are doing your best with what you know (just as our parents did).

So, as we finish this chapter, where I have taken you on a bit of a historical journey, I encourage you to reflect on the chapter tile - Parenting: Job or Journey and stow it away in the back of your mind and revisit it every so often as we move through the coming pages and chapters.

And with that, I'll see you over the page.

# Chapter 2

# Nurturing Potential: Brain Development Through The First 1000 Days and Beyond

*"The most important thing that parents need to understand is that the brain of their child will become exactly what the child was exposed to …That is the beauty of the human brain, it is the mirror the child's developmental experience."*
— *Dr Bruce Perry*

So, we've had the history lesson. It is now time for the science lesson, once a teacher always a teacher, I guess! No seriously, to set the scene for you and provide some foundational learning of human development, it is essential to consider the science that sits behind it. Don't panic, I will not get all scientific and use a bunch of fancy words that neither of us understand, because, well I'm not a neuroscientist!

If we have a little understanding of human development, it will help us navigate what our kids need from us from the very moment of conception, yes you read that correctly, from conception! Did you know an unborn child can be impacted by any stress (maternal stress) that the mother experiences? Stress from the outside world can be passed on to the baby in the womb, because at the risk of stating the obvious, a mother provides the physiological space for her unborn child to grow. This becomes particularly concerning when a mother is exposed to high and prolonged levels of stress, which can lead to increased levels of the stress hormone, cortisol. High levels of cortisol can impact an unborn child's brain architecture development, reduce brain size, shape and structure, and can lead to impaired functioning as a child grows and develops. Sobering isn't it!

Hence the reason I wanted to talk about how critical the first 1000 days of a child's life or roughly the first 2 years are. The first 1000 days is where the rubber really hits the road for our little people. Now just to be clear, it's not strictly from conception to 2 and it's not like, once the 2 year mark has been reached that the box is ticked and we move to the next milestone. Because as you know, as humans we are unique and our children will reach milestones on their very own schedule, not one we devise for them.

Humans are born with over 100 billion brain cells or neurons, as they are known scientifically, and we do not grow any more as we age. To get a handle on that number of neurons, it is about 20 times the number of people on the planet or about 10 times more stars than in the entire milky way.

*Nurturing Potential: Brain Development*

Now imagine our brains are like supercomputers, and the neurons are its tiny building blocks. The neurons are the special cells that send and receive messages, a lot like how our phones enable us to send texts to each other.

When babies are born, they have an extraordinary amount of neurons (100 billion), but they're not all connected yet. Think of it like a puzzle that needs to be put together. As babies grow and learn, their brains build connections between these neurons. It's like creating roads between different cities on a map. These connections are called synaptic activity and these experiences shape and form the architecture of the brain.

Every time a baby sees, hears, or touches something, their neurons make new connections and it's these connections that help them learn about the world. For example, when a baby touches something soft, their neurons make a connection that says, *soft things feel nice.*

As babies keep exploring and learning, some connections get stronger, while others fade away if they're not used. It's like the more you use a path, the clearer and stronger it becomes. This process helps babies develop skills like talking, walking, and even understanding emotions.

The image below shows the synaptic density of the human brain at birth through to 15 years of age.

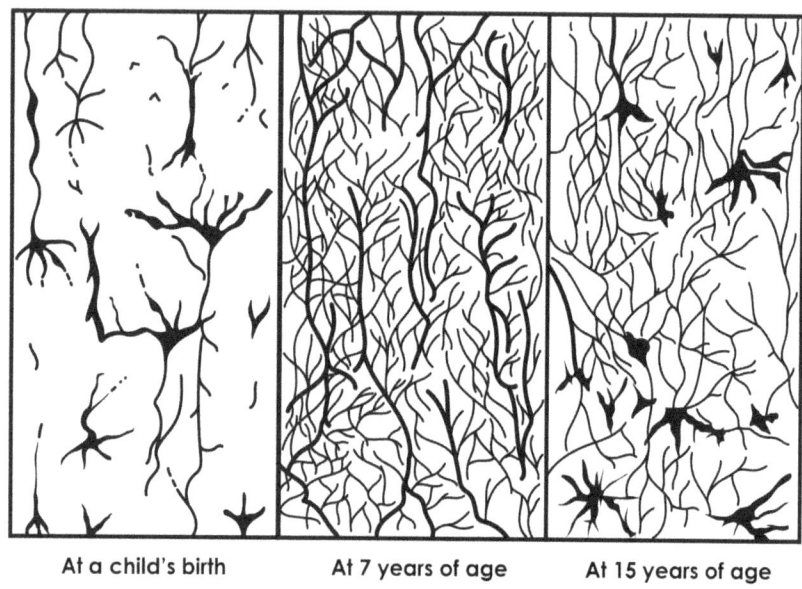

| At a child's birth | At 7 years of age | At 15 years of age |

Ways to nuture a child's mental health

Sean Brotherson a Family Science Specialist at the North Dakota State University states:

> *"By the time a child is 3 years old, a baby's brain has formed about 1,000 trillion connections — about twice as many as adults have. A baby's brain is superdense and will stay that way throughout the first decade of life. Beginning at about age 11, a child's brain gets rid of extra connections in a process calling 'pruning,' gradually making order out of a thick tangle of 'wires.'"* [2]

## Nurturing Potential: Brain Development

You'd have to agree that is an astonishing number, and I think it's important for us to take a moment and appreciate the incredible brilliance of the brain. Its capacity to prune away unused connections, clearing space for more crucial connections to thrive and grow, is nothing short of magnificent.

To demonstrate further how crazy good our brains are, did you know?

Our brain actually produces enough electricity to power a lightbulb. You know those cartoons where characters get a bright idea and a lightbulb pops up above their heads? Well, guess what – your brain could technically light up a lightbulb for real.

Here's another cool bit of information: our brain is about 80% liquid. That's why it's so important to stay hydrated and drink plenty of water. When we're dehydrated, our brain doesn't work as well, so keep that water bottle handy.

And get this: the neurons in our brain are like speed demons. They zip around transmitting information at speeds of over 240 kilometres per hour (that's around 149 miles per hour!). Why? Because sometimes our body needs to react super-fast to things, like when you accidentally touch a hot pan – your hand jerks away before you even have time to think. It's all about those quick reflexes keeping us out of harm's way.

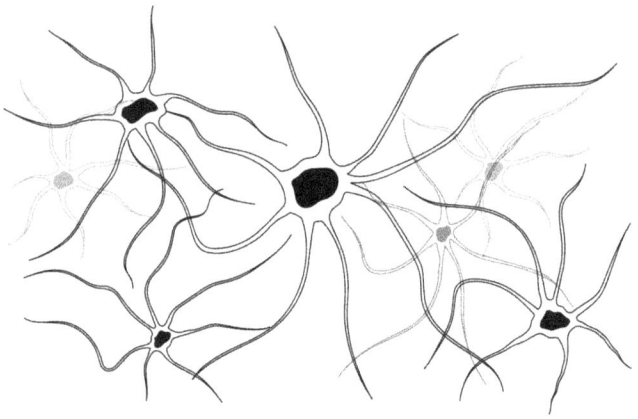

Neurons: Essential for the nervous system, driving communication, processing information, memory, motor control, and sensory perception.

As you can see, there is A LOT going in our heads, and I don't mean the stuff we are conscious of, such as what you are having for dinner tonight or how annoyed you are that you didn't get the job you wanted. The activity I am referring to here is the speed demons zooming around, transmitting information and guiding our body and its responses.

Picture the experience for our babies and toddlers, who, in a sense, start with a clean slate. Contemplate how much data their developing brains are processing! All the noises, smells, tastes, sights and touch they experience in those early days. Miraculous hey! You can probably tell by now I tend to 'geek out' on neuroscience.

During the first 1000 days the brain is at its peak plasticity. The brain is at its most flexible, impressionable, and is shaped by *experience* and *environment* and it is growing like crazy.

At this point, you might be curious about what all of this means for you as a parent, grandparent, or anyone who may be caring for a young child. By simply staying with me through this straightforward science lesson (no judgment, I'm a generalist teacher by profession), my hope is you have a greater understanding of brain development and function, and what is physiologically happening inside your little one's brain at any given point. Parenting with the brain in mind, is a powerful approach that can have lasting positive outcomes.

'Parenting with the brain in mind' is a term coined by one of my all-time favourite neuroscientist's Dr Dan Siegel(2011). Dr Dan is a clinical professor of psychiatry at the UCLA School of Medicine and executive director of the Mindsight Institute.

Here is what he says about the importance of parents knowing a little about their child's brain:

> *"...since the brain itself is significantly shaped by the experiences we offer as parents, knowing about the way the brain changes in response to our parenting can help us to nurture a stronger more resilient child"* [3]

and he goes on to say:

> *"... by understanding a few simple and easy to master basics about how the brain works, you'll be able to better understand your child, respond more effectively to difficult situations and build a foundation for social, emotional and mental health".* [4]

Easy right! Well, yes, and no, because there is a wee bit more to knowing about the brain and the way it works. The good news is if we combine the knowledge above with an understanding of a process called integration, then we can completely transform the way we think about parenting and being with our kids. So rather than immediately thinking, *'oh man this has turned to sh!t what am I going to do?'* we can use our new knowledge and understanding to buy ourselves some time to be with our kids rather than react to them when things get wobbly.

As you know the brain is divided into two halves but has many parts to it and each part has a role to play and job to do.

Let's take a quick look at each of the parts:

**Left Hemisphere** - Typically associated with analytical and logical thinking. Functions and characteristics of the left brain include:

- Language processing: responsible for speech and understanding language.
- Analytical Thinking: known for its ability to break down complex information into smaller parts.
- Sequential processing: helps us to follow step by step instructions.
- Fine Motor Skills: plays a role in controlling fine motor movements, such as writing and intricate tasks.
- Verbal Memory: involved in storing and retrieving verbal information such as names, addresses and facts.

**Right Hemisphere** - Often associated with holistic and creative thinking functions and characteristics of the right brain include:

*Nurturing Potential: Brain Development*

- Spatial Awareness: excels at perceiving and understanding spatial relationships, which are important for tasks like reading maps, navigating through a space.
- Visual Processing: responsible for processing visual information, including recognising faces and interpreting non-verbal cues such as body language and facial expressions.
- Creativity and Imagination: linked to creativity, artistic abilities, and imaginative thinking. It helps us see the big picture and make connections between seemingly unrelated concepts.
- Emotional Processing: plays a key role in processing and expressing emotions. It contributes to our ability to understand the emotions of others and interpret emotional subtleties.
- Holistic Thinking: processes information in a more holistic and context-driven manner, allowing us to understand situations in their entirety.
- Gestural Communication: contributes to understanding and producing non-verbal communication, such as gestures and body language.

**Left brain**
Analytical/Logical
- Speech
- Analytical thinking
- Sequencing
- Following instructions
- Fine motor skills
- Memory

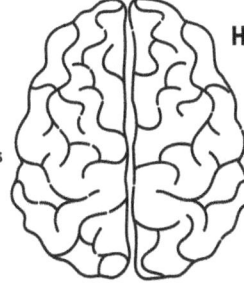

**Right brain**
Holistic/Creative/ Emotions
- Spatial awareness
- Visual processory
- Imagination
- Creativity
- Emotion
- Facial recognition
- Big picture thinking
- Intuition
- Non verbal communication

So once again you are probably thinking (using the left side of your brain), why is this important and how will it make my parenting journey more meaningful and manageable?

The answers lay within the process of integration. The aim of integration is to have all the parts of your child's brain working well together, in harmony, rather than resembling a symphony without a conductor, playing disjointed notes, each instrument out of tune creating a cacophony of confusion.

Dr Dan Seigel (2011) 2011 explains it like this:

> *"That's what integration does: it coordinates and balances the separate regions of the brain that link together. It's easy to see when our kids aren't integrated - they become overwhelmed by their emotions, confused and chaotic. They can't respond calmly and capably to the situation at hand. Tantrums, meltdowns, aggression and most of the other challenging experiences of parenting - and life - are the result of a loss of integration, also known as dis- integration".*[5]

It's important to remember that everyday parenting challenges and struggles with our kids is a result of a lack of integration within a child's brain. It is not just them waking up in the morning and planning how many times they are going to p!ss you off that day. The simple truth behind it is a child's brain has not had time to develop yet, in fact, the science tells us that a brain doesn't fully develop until a person reaches their mid-twenties! But somehow we expect our 3 year old kids to manage a whole range of experiences in an adult-like way.

## Nurturing Potential: Brain Development

With that being said, let's think back on what we've talked about so far. We know that the brain has billions of neurons firing off and when they fire together, they make new connections, shaping the brain's architecture. But the most critical thing to remember here is that experience and environments moulds the brain. The experiences and environments parents provide and expose their child to facilitates the constant wiring and rewiring of the brain because of its plasticity. Every experience we have shapes the development of our brain.

This applies to healthy and nurturing experiences and environments as well as exposure to any adverse and prolonged experiences such as violence, substance abuse and mental health issues. Those types of negative experiences all cause toxic stress that impacts the developing brain in a lasting way.

Experiences and environments occur every single day, often multiple times throughout a day; think sibling fights, tantrums, meltdowns and sandwiches cut into squares, not triangles. Thank goodness, there is always an opportunity to practice and support integration for both you and your child, cause let's face it, adults can also be disintegrated at times too.

What does it look like?

Dr Dan Seigel talks about us having our own proverbial 'little canoe in the river of wellbeing'. When we (our canoe) are in the flow (integrated) there is harmony, and we are feeling safe, secure and stable. It is only when our canoe drifts towards the banks of the river of wellbeing that things get wobbly. On one side of the river is the bank of rigidity and the other is the bank of chaos. It's when our kids crash into a bank (aka lose their sh!t) we see it play out right in front of us and it can sometimes happen in the blink of an eye. I think we've all seen our kids go from 0 to 100 in one second flat and wonder what the hell happened!

Rigidity looks like:

Your 3 year old won't share his toy boat at the park…

Chaos looks like:

He erupts into crying, yelling and throwing sand when his new friend takes the boat away.

It's in the heat of this moment, under our own integration stress, with other parents looking on thinking, *how is she going to handle this?*, where we decide how to respond. And speaking from experience I have responded to similar situations in so many different ways, including raising my voice, issuing threats, such as, *'that's it. We are never coming back to the playground ever again',* physically removing my child from a situation, using shame. Oh and we can't forget the countdown, I always started at five cause it gave me what I thought was more time to get the outcome I was seeking and would save me a ton of embarrassment and judgment if I was in a public place.

They were all strategies that I had at my disposal, but hand on heart strategies that always left me feeling like I hadn't handled the situation well and my child was on the end of it feeling horrible too.

It was only when I learned about brain development and understood the concepts of rigidity and chaos, was I able to think differently about my child's responses and their reactions to things and the surrounding environment. So rather than reacting to a situation, I trained myself to observe and view the behaviour through the lens of; my child's nervous system is feeling threatened, which is leading them to respond in a disintegrated way, how can I support them? Granted it took a whole heap of practice and many trip ups from me along the way, but it was so worth the investment in the practice as I felt calmer and a little more in control when things went pear shaped.

Well, that brings us to the end of the science lesson, with the aim of this chapter being to introduce you to the concept of parenting with the brain in mind. I hope it has encouraged and empowered you to think about what it might mean and look like for you now and into the future of your parenting journey. The good news is, we will explore this some more in the next chapter with a focus on supporting our kids' emotional landscape, leading to connection, belonging, and secure attachment.

See you over the page.

# Chapter 3

# Growing Your Child's Happy Emotional World: The Key Ingredient

*"The propensity to make strong bonds to particular individuals (is) a basic component of human nature."*
— *John Bowlby (2006)*

I clearly remember those early days of my parenting journey when I was still in the bubble of love and had a vision of myself being the perfect Mum and having the skills to navigate all that would come my way. Remember I had five years of teaching experience to my name!

I also remember just as clearly when the realisation hit me, like a punch to my stomach, that I didn't always have the answers. On so many occasions, I didn't know what to do or would often think, what the hell do I do here or how do I help my son?

Without a doubt, my husband and I muddled along and did what we thought was right, but we also spent a significant amount of time in a state of constant worry. We'd worry about so many things with our firstborn (and second); was he warm enough, will he hit all the milestones at the 'right' time, are we good enough parents, is he going to grow up and go rogue, are we giving him enough attention, are we giving him too much attention, is he safe, will we hurt him or let him down or that we'd worry that we'd worry too much, crazy hey! There are so many more things that we worried about, too many to list here, in fact I reckon I could complete an entire chapter on it.

But I also think we are not alone here, every parent especially those that are committed, intentional and thoughtful (like you, otherwise you wouldn't have picked up my book) could fill in the blanks with something they worry about on the daily. I believe it's fair to say we all succumb at different times to the feeling of anxiety and not being a good enough parent.

My wish for you for this chapter, is that by the end, you will know that just by caring deeply about your child and being an imperfect parent is, in fact, PERFECT. But to make it even more perfect for you, I am going to share the answer to the question you have been patiently waiting on: how do I help my kid to be happy, healthy and emotionally connected?

The reason I say share is that the answer lies within the research and science conducted by my favourite neuroscientist, Dr Dan Seigel and Tina Bryson, a psychotherapist, when they address the question:

> *"What's the single most important thing I can do for my kids to help them succeed and feel at home in the world? Our answer is simple (but not necessarily easy): Show up for your kids."* [6]

Boom! There it is. The answer is to just *show up* for your kids.

It's the one tool in your tool kit that is always at your disposal. When you are not sure how to respond and things are about to, or have already gone pear shaped, instead of worrying or trying to find the perfect solution or to be the perfect parent, just *show up*.

Dr Dan Seigel and Tina Bryson (2020) explain showing up this way:

> *"Showing up means what it sounds like. It means being there for you kids, it means being physically present, as well as providing a quality of presence… "*

> *"Showing up means bringing your whole being - your attention and awareness - when you're with your child. When we show up, we are mentally and emotionally present for our child at that moment."* [7]

Pretty powerful stuff, isn't it?

We are in charge of how we show up. Consistently showing up, will empower you and your child. It will promote their ability to bounce back and build emotional strength even if we muck it up on a regular basis.

Now it has to be said here and acknowledged that depending on your background and how you experienced being parented, *showing up* for your kids may or may not come naturally to you and that's ok. Because even if you recognise that you aren't currently or don't know how to show up for your kids, have compassion for yourself and remember, good enough parenting is good enough, and it's never too late.

Leaning once again on the research of Dr Dan Seigel and Tina Bryson PhD (2020) to further explain the power of showing up they state:

> *"The longitudinal research on child development clearly demonstrates that one of the very best predictors for how any child turns out - in terms of happiness, social and emotional development, leaderships skills, meaningful relationships and academic and career success - is whether they developed security from having at least one person who showed up for them. Across cultures around the globe, these studies reveal a universal finding about how we can parent well, if not flawlessly."* [8]

So regardless of your current understanding or ability to show up for your kids, this chapter will provide you with some information that gets right to the heart of what showing up looks like, feels like, and sounds like. And what I am hoping is one of your key takeaways will be; consistently but imperfectly showing up for your child holds the key to building a secure trust based emotional attachment with your child that will support them to be happy, and emotionally connected human beings.

## Growing Your Child's Happy Emotional World: The Key Ingredient

*Ok so what does it look like, sound like, feel like and what is the outcome?*

To get us started, I'll share with you the four pillars that underpin the showing up model, that when practiced, leads to our kids developing a secure attachment to a parent who predictably (but not perfectly) cares for them.

Dr Dan Seigel and Tina Bryson call them the **Four S's** - helping kids feel:

1. *Safe - they feel protected and sheltered from harm.*
2. *Seen – they know you care about them and pay attention to them.*
3. *Soothed – they know you'll be there for them when they are hurting.*
4. *Secure - based on the other S's, they trust you to predictably help them feel 'at home' in the world, then learn to help themselves feel safe, seen and soothed.* [9]

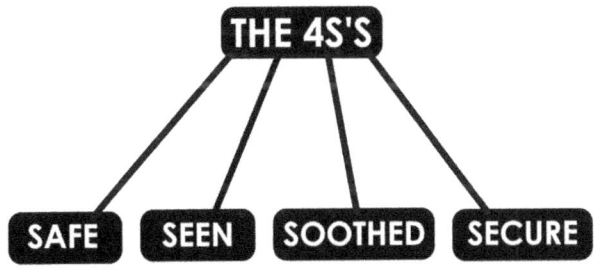

This is where our knowledge from the previous chapter about brain development and integration comes into play. As you'll recall, every experience we have shapes the development of the brain. If we as parents consistently show up for our kids, the little neurons in their brains are firing off, building those connections, shaping and moulding the brain's architecture, to where our kids' minds come to expect that the world is a place where they are, safe, seen, soothed and secure, which leads to secure attachment - the ultimate goal for a parent.

Every time you comfort or boost your child's confidence, you're building a bond of trust between the two of you. When you show that you truly understand how they feel and what they want, you're providing the strong, hard wired need for connection that we all seek right from birth. And helping your baby or toddler deal with the challenges of being new to the world teaches them how to handle their own emotions and be understanding of other people feelings.

The 4S's of secure attachment and supporting your child's ability to integrate are the gifts we can give our kids during everyday moments, that may seem forgettable or mundane, but when accumulated, they accrue to be nothing short of profound to our kids' sense of connection and belonging.

Let's walk through each of the pillars and look at some practical, easy ways to show up for your kids.

## *Pillar 1: Safe*

An absolute non-negotiable for all our kids is the innate need to feel safe, physically, emotionally and relationally. This is perhaps the most important pillar in the foundation of the emotional house in which our kids are going to reside in for the rest of their lives. They need to feel and know that they are safe and that their parents will be there to protect them from physical harm, but also keep them safe emotionally and relationally.

Now that bar feels incredibly high when spelt out like that in black and white on the page, but as frequently mentioned in previous chapters, we are all human and we are going to make mistakes and mess things up, or our kids mess things up with us, however there is always time and opportunity to repair. Repairing the rupture as soon as possible enables our kids to learn that even though mistakes are made, or unkind things are said and done, we still love each other and want to set things right again.

So as difficult as it can be sometimes, when our child is challenging us and we lose our sh!t, and respond in a way that makes them feel unsafe, for example yelling or making threats, apologising can be the superhighway back to restoring the connection and a sense of safety for your child.

It's also important for us to understand here that we do not want to be a source of fear for our kids, as this leads to disorganised attachment, which severely impacts our kids' sense of safety.

To explain a little further, disorganised attachment is an insecure relationship style that some children develop with their parent or caregiver. It arises when a parent's behaviour is unpredictable or even frightening, leading to mixed feelings of fear and attachment. For example, if a child's parent sometimes comforts them but other times scares them with angry outbursts, the child may exhibit disorganised attachment, feeling both drawn to and fearful of their parent. This confusion can result from traumatic experiences, caregiver mental health issues, or unstable family environments, causing the child to have difficulties forming a consistent and secure emotional bond.

*Beyond Bottles Baths and Bed*

It's also important to call out here that life is hard and many people are dealt some terrible hands throughout their lives, so while our behaviour and responses as parents and adults is critical to our children, our life experiences have also impacted and shaped our brains. Thankfully, most adults are not intentionally malicious, they may just be struggling with their own challenges and issues that affect their parenting behaviour.

Compassion rather than judgment is required in these instances, as I truly believe, no parent wants to be a source of fear for the child. They are responding in the best way they know how.

### Pillar 2: Seen

When we think about showing up and what it might mean for our kids to be seen - we think about being physically present. Such as going to the park with them, reading a book together or sitting on the lounge together watching television. Whilst these things are important to build connection, what the pillar of being seen actually means is that we focus on what is really happening on the inside for our little people. Being seen to our kids means we attune to their inner feelings and thoughts, and really notice what their nervous systems are telling us underneath the behaviours that we can see.

It means paying attention to their emotions, good, bad and ugly. Of course, we can't do that every minute of the day, but if we celebrate with them when they succeed at something they have worked at or hurt with them when they have a fall or are 'rejected' by a friend, then we are tuning into their inner landscape. That's what it means to show up for them emotionally and relationally. When we are attuned, this is when our kids come to '*feel felt*', when they truly know that we have a sense of what is happening for them on the inside. If our kids *feel felt*, we are helping those neurons fire off and "*neurons that fire together wire together*"[10] as coined by neuropsychologist Donald Hebb in 1949, when he was explaining how neural pathways in the brain are established and strengthened by repetition. Creating strong neural pathways is critical to developing a deep sense of security and connection.

*Beyond Bottles Baths and Bed*

## *Pillar 3: Soothed*

The Oxford dictionary describes being soothed as: *"gently calm (a person or their feelings)."* But what does it mean for our kids? It means our kids feel safe, secure, and at ease during their toughest, most challenging times. What it doesn't mean is that we rescue them from all discomfort and wrap them in bubble wrap to avoid all pain. In fact, these are the moments when our kids will learn and grow the most. It is during these times where we need to allow our kids to experience the trials and tribulations of life such as: not being able to have that extra lolly at snack time, or being unable to complete the puzzle after multiple attempts, or becoming frustrated with not being able to tie their shoe lace, or when conflict arises with siblings and friends.

These experiences are all about teaching them that, yes they are angry, hurt, annoyed or frustrated, (fill in the blank), but it is ok to feel those feels and that you will be there to support them to ride the waves when they come along. It is critical our kids are never in any doubt about whether we will show up during the hard times, they will know in the very deepest part of their core that you will be there to provide comfort and support and that they will never have to suffer alone.

## Pillar 4: Security

When we put all the pillars together and our kids are feeling safe, seen and soothed, they come to feeling secure, as they become securely attached.

Feeling securely attached comes with predictability and knowing that their adult will show up for them time and time again. However, we are all human and we're going to make mistakes, there is no such thing as perfection and getting it right every time.

But what it is about, is letting your child know they can count on you to be there, time after time after time. Their security will grow and embed when time and time again you do all that you can to make them feel *safe*, you'll do all you can to make them *feel felt* and when things get a bit wobbly or completely pear shaped, you will be there to *soothe* and comfort, leading to the ultimate goal of secure attachment.

### Secure attachment - Why is it so important?

I'm guessing you are getting a real sense of what underpins our kids' emotional landscape but indulge me as I reiterate why secure attachment matters a lot.

It's like the emotional glue between kids and their parents. It's the bond that shapes how they will handle their feelings, explore the world, and deal with stress. When our kids feel safe, they're more confident to learn and discover. It's this deep connection that sticks with them as they grow, affecting how they see themselves and others. It's linked to them having good self-esteem, being able to cope under pressure, developing friendships and maintaining strong relationships. It sets the scene for the rest of their life, so doing our best for our kids right from the beginning is crucial to their development from birth to adulthood.

**That's why it is so important.**

To further illustrate the importance, over 50 years of research into secure attachment reveals the following benefits for kids:

- Enjoy more happiness with their parents
- Feel less anger at their parents
- Get along better with friends
- Have stronger friendships
- Are able to solve a problem with friends
- Have better relationships with brothers and sisters
- Have higher self esteem
- Know that most problems will have an answer
- Trust that good things will come their way
- Trust people they love
- Know how to be kind to those around them

The magic ingredient lies in the phenomenal collective impact of the 4S's on the brain, which serves to help our kids maintain their integration. Each pillar, combined with the other, works to ensure that our kids don't experience prolonged stress and they move about in the world working on the premise that they are loved, safe and have relationships they can rely on. They have the skills to navigate life's tricky moments and have a sense of connection, belonging, and security in the world.

Disclaimer: the information discussed above is not the magic bullet and is not designed to be a formula to follow step by step. Our kids are all amazing little individuals who come to us with a very unique set of DNA, which includes temperament and genetic predisposition to a range of traits, characteristics and conditions. But what the information shared in this chapter can do is provide us with the knowledge, skills and tools we can use to support our kids in the moment. We know what the science tells us works and it can be applied in any situation with any child or adult for that matter. At the very core of this information is we just have to remember that our kids need us to show up for them, time and time again because as we also know; life is not always unicorns and rainbows.

See you over the page!

# Chapter 4

# Showing Up: What Impacts our Ability?

*"Pooh?" whispered Piglet.*
*"Yes, Piglet?" said Pooh.*
*"Oh, nothing," said Piglet.*
*"I was just making sure of you." (AA Milne)*

We have talked a lot about how critical it is to our kids that we show up for them and we've seen what that looks like and the benefits of showing up.

The intention behind this chapter is to present a well-rounded perspective on parenting, offering insight into the reasons behind our parenting behaviours. It also aims to highlight obstacles that hinder our effective presence as parents and how these factors can influence the future lives of our children as they grow into adults.

It's complex and I will touch on a few only, as it's a PhD body of work that requires a significant amount of time to unpack and it is quite heavy going.

I want to say before moving on though, is that there is no judgment about why some parents don't or can't show up for their kids. As we know, our brains are shaped by experience and environment and reflect our childhood attachment patterns, and compassion for oneself is always the key.

Let's jump in…

### How childhood attachment patterns impact how we parent:

We were all children once and how we were parented and the experiences and environments that we were exposed to provide us with an attachment history. Attachment scientists have created names for the adult attachment patterns that relate to childhood experiences and patterns. As we talk about each of the attachment categories, you may resonate with elements of a category. You may also find yourself reflecting on how your childhood attachment history is coming through in the way you parent now.

### Secure and Free Attachment:

Secure and free attachment category is what scientists call the adult version of secure attachment. This category refers to what adult relationships look like based on early attachment patterns and is characterised by the person having a sense of safety and trust in relationships, enabling emotional vulnerability and effective communication.

Securely attached individuals form healthy, balanced connections, and are comfortable with intimacy, can manage conflicts constructively, and are open to seeking and offering support. The adult category of secure and free attachment captures the essence of healthy adult relationships, emphasising the importance of feeling secure, emotionally supported, and empowered to express one's individuality within the context of a loving partnership.

Parents that have a childhood history of secure attachment are more likely to show up for their own kids as they are more attuned and responsive to their kids' needs for connection and sense of belonging.

### *Insecure: Avoidant Attachment*

The avoidant attachment category refers to a relational pattern where individuals struggle with forming close emotional bonds due to past experiences of inconsistent caregiving.

These experiences often lead to a defensive coping strategy characterised by emotional distance and self-sufficiency. Adults with avoidant attachment downplay their own emotions and needs, preferring independence and self-reliance. They may find it challenging to openly express vulnerability or seek support from others, fearing that intimacy could lead to disappointment or rejection. This attachment style can hinder the development of deep, meaningful relationships, as the individual's inclination to maintain emotional distance may inadvertently create barriers to genuine connection.

A parent with an avoidant attachment history is more likely to be indifferent to their child's needs and signals for connection, they lack the ability to tune into their child's emotional needs, as it was absent in their own childhood. They do not know what or how it feels to be attuned.

## *Insecure: Ambivalent Attachment*

Ambivalent attachment in adults originates from early caregiving experiences marked by inconsistency and unpredictability. A parent with ambivalent attachment displays inconsistent and unpredictable caregiving behaviours towards their child due to their own unresolved childhood attachment issues. These parents may fluctuate between being overly involved and emotionally distant, which causes confusion for the child. They often struggle to meet their child's emotional needs consistently, resulting in the child feeling uncertain about their parent's availability and responsiveness. This can lead to the child developing anxiety and a heightened need for reassurance.

The parent with an ambivalent attachment history is sometimes attuned and responsive to their child's needs and sometimes not, causing confusion for the child.

## *Insecure: Disorganised Attachment*

A parent with disorganised attachment exhibits erratic and unpredictable behaviours towards their child because of their own traumatic experiences or unresolved emotional issues. This attachment style often leads to confusing and contradictory caregiving responses. They may show both nurturing and frightening behaviours, leaving the child uncertain about how to seek comfort or safety. Children of parents with disorganised attachment often struggle to develop an understanding of relationships and emotions. As adults, they might face challenges in forming stable and healthy connections, as their early experiences may have left them with a lack of clear models for safe attachment.

In short, a parent with a disorganised attachment childhood history can significantly struggle to attune to their child's needs and signals for connection and can be a source of terror and confusion.

The table I've included below by Dr Dan Seigel and Tina Bryson. PhD is set out in an easy to read way and provides an overview of the various attachment patterns, the parenting tendencies and the child assumptions.

| Child Attachment Pattern | Parenting Tendencies | Child's Wired Assumptions |
|---|---|---|
| Secure | Secure attachment. Pattern: Sensitive, attuned, responsive to baby's bid for connection: an ability to read child's cues and predictably meet child's needs. Parents reliably *show up* for child | My parent isn't perfect, but I know I am safe. If I have a need, she will see it and respond quickly and sensitively. I can trust that other people will do that too. My inner experiences is real and worthy of being expressed and respected. |
| Insecure: Avoidant | Dismissing attachment. Pattern: Indifference to child's signals and needs; lack of attunement to child's emotional needs | My parent may be around a lot but he doesn't care about what I need or how I feel, so I'll learn to ignore my emotions and avoid communicating my needs. |
| Insecure: Ambivalent | Preoccupied attachment. Pattern: Sometimes attuned, sensitive and responsive to child's signals and needs and sometimes not. Sometimes intrusive. | I never know how my parent will respond, so I have to stay constantly on edge. I can't ever let my guard down. I can't trust that people will predictably be there for me. |

| Insecure: Disorganised | Unresolved attachment. Pattern: severely unattuned to child's signals and needs; disorienting, either frightening, frightened, or both. | My parent is terrifying and disorienting. I am not safe and there is no one to keep me safe. I don't know what to do. I am helpless. People are scary and unpredictable. |

There is some great easy to understand information included in the table, that I hope clarifies the science behind each of the attachment patterns for adults and kids.

Along with understanding parenting tendencies, it is important to touch on how balancing technology and parenting has become an important and complex aspect of modern parenting, especially when it interferes with our ability to show up for our kids.

## Connected but Disconnected

In a world where we are the MOST connected we have ever been in the history of time (think technology), it is also a time where we are at risk of being the most disconnected. Bit of a mind bending concept that one isn't it? What I am suggesting here is that our obsession with our phones and addiction to social media is having profound impacts on us human beings.

If we consider our (the royal 'our' as I acknowledge this is not all adults) obsession with devices through the lens of 'showing up', there are a number of implications for our kids, including:

- **Limited Quality Time**: when parents are frequently engrossed in their devices, they can potentially miss opportunities for meaningful interactions and quality time with their kids.
- **Modelling Behaviour:** parents serve as role models for their children. If kids observe their parents using phones excessively, they may learn that it's acceptable to prioritise screens over face-to-face interactions or other activities.
- **Decline in Communication Skills**: kids learn language, communication, and social skills by interacting with their caregivers. When parents are constantly on their devices, there are potentially fewer opportunities for kids and parents to engage in meaningful conversations and learn these important skills.
- **Increased Behavioural Issues:** kids might resort to attention-seeking behaviours or act out in order to gain their parents' attention if they feel neglected because of device use.
- **Role Reversal:** sometimes, when parents are consistently absorbed in their devices, older kids might feel like they have to take on a caregiving role to get their parents' attention.
- **Miscommunication:** misunderstandings can arise when parents are not fully engaged during conversations because of device distractions, potentially leading to communication breakdowns.

Each of these examples gives us a snapshot into how technology and devices can impede our ability to fully show up. So how might we mitigate these potential impacts?

*Showing Up: What Impacts our Ability?*

It's as simple as being more mindful of device use and establishing healthy boundaries by:

- **Designating Screen-Free Times**: set specific times when the family is device-free, such as during meals, family outings, or before bedtime.
- **Modelling Healthy Behaviour**: show children the importance of balanced device use by engaging in activities that don't involve screens.
- **Creating Tech-Free Zones**: designate certain areas in the home, such as bedrooms, as tech-free zones to promote relaxation and healthy sleep.
- **Actively Listening:** when spending time with your child, actively engage in conversations, listen attentively, and show genuine interest. This is showing them that you see them and feel them.
- **Prioritising Quality Time:** dedicate focused time for bonding activities that promote positive interactions and emotional connections.

Now the intent of raising the technology issue was not for anyone reading this to beat themselves up if they've accidentally slipped into the habit of being connected to their phone a little more often than not. It's more of a gentle reminder that our devices can steal our time by stealth, but there are some easy ways for us to get our time back and show up for our kids when they need us.

To further demonstrate how much our kids need us to be present, I wanted to share with you an experiment that was first conducted over 50 years ago but is still as relevant now as it was way back then. The experiment called the 'Still Face Experiment' clearly shows what it physically looks like and feels like when we don't attune to our kids' needs, even when they are trying their hardest to get us to show up for them.

### *The Still Face Experiment:*

When I first saw the Still Face experiment, it made me shift uncomfortably in my seat and at times made me feel quite distressed. It had a profound impact on the way I understood what babies needed from their parents to feel connected and safe. The Still Face video is also a very powerful depiction of both what connection looks like for our kids and what it looks like and feels like when they don't get what they need from us.

I'll provide you with an overview of the Still Face Experiment here, but strongly encourage you to check out the video and watch for yourself. Link to the video will be provided at the back of the book in the references section.

The Still Face Experiment was conducted by developmental psychologist Dr. Edward Tronick in the 1970s and is a landmark study illustrating the critical role of parent responsiveness to infant development. The experiment highlighted how disruptions in parent-infant interactions can profoundly impact emotional well-being.

The experiment involved three phases. In the initial phase, the parent and the infant engage in typical back-and-forth interactions, also known as serve and return interactions, creating a sense of emotional connection. This interactive exchange established the foundation of trust and security for the infant.

*Showing Up: What Impacts our Ability?*

The second phase is the 'still-face' phase. And this is where things become difficult to watch in the video. It's in this phase that the caregiver suddenly presents a neutral and an unresponsive facial expression, withholding any interaction from the infant. This abrupt shift in behaviour creates a stark contrast to the previously engaging interactions. The infant who is accustomed to responsive exchanges, reacts with confusion and distress. The infant displays various attempts to regain the caregiver's attention—smiling, cooing, gesturing—to restore the familiar interaction pattern. But when the child does not get the connection they are seeking, the distress in the child escalates to a point of crying and moving their body to trigger a response from the parent.

The final phase of the experiment involves the parent resuming normal interactions with the infant. Which typically sees the infant react with relief, seeking to reconnect with the parent. The experiment showed that even a brief interruption of responsiveness during the still-face phase can disrupt the infant's emotional equilibrium. The distress experienced in this phase reflects the infant's reliance on consistent caregiver engagement for emotional regulation and security. That is, consistently and predictably showing up time and time again.

The Still Face Experiment vividly demonstrates how parents' interactions lay the foundation for a child's emotional resilience and social competence. It also highlights the critical role of consistent and attuned 'showing up' for promoting healthy emotional development and the establishment of secure attachment between parents and kids.

Whilst this chapter hasn't been all light and rainbows, I hope it has given an insight into why some people parent like they do, as well as provided you with a little more understanding of how and why you might parent like you do. I also hope that by highlighting how technology can hijack our time, by stealth, it may have raised some awareness as to how we can mitigate usage and get back some time to increase connection with our kids and loved ones.

If you would like to learn some more about each of the adult attachment styles, there is a huge amount of information out there, but I highly recommend the work of Dr Dan Seigel, Kent Hoffman, Glen Cooper and Bert Powell, all experts in the field of attachment.

The underlying message here also is that there is no judgment, only compassion and imperfect parenting is the goal we should be striving for us and for our kids. Regardless of your childhood attachment history, I want to leave you with a quote by Dr Dan Siegel and Tina Bryson PhD (2020):

> *"History is NOT destiny. By making sense of your own story, you can be the kind of parent you want to be - regardless of how you were parented."* [11]

See you over the page.

# Chapter 5

# Regulation: The Key to Taming Big Emotions

*"Emotion is at the core of every child"*
- Gurudev Sri Ravi Shankar

If ever there were a million opportunities to show up and support your child's emotional landscape, it is during the period of time following the Wonderful Ones! There will be multiple times during the Threenager years, Effing Fours, Fantastic Fives or the Snarky Sixes and beyond, to put on your bravest face and show up.

These years are the time of growth where we get to experience it ALL with our kids. They are incredibly open to sharing their opinions on how they feel about all things related to them and their need for that extra piece of chocolate that you just know is going to tip them over the edge!

It is also the period of time that we can be most challenged by our kids' behaviour and a time when our responses are most critical in supporting the foundation of secure attachment.

Those of you who have children already can probably relate to the feelings that bubble up inside of you when your little Miss Three engages in a dramatic performance, worthy of an Oscar, just because she doesn't want to leave the playground yet. Or Mr Four, who shouts at you in the supermarket that you are the meanest mum of all time, because you won't fulfill his need for the pack of twelve cupcakes on the end of an aisle. It sends shivers, doesn't it?

For those of you yet to experience the joy of the above, rest assured you will at some stage, but lucky for you, you will be a little forewarned and forearmed with the information included in this chapter.

But the most reassuring thing about these moments that we endure or rejoice in is that it is developmentally perfect. If your little person is throwing a tantrum, melting down or throwing you a bit of sass on the regular, be grateful, as their responses are exactly where they should be. Tantrums plus other similar responses, whilst challenging, are part of age-appropriate brain development and are all markers that paediatricians or GPs look for should you need to visit them. It's certainly not a sign of bad parenting or that your child is the spawn of the devil. Most kids experience this stage, so you're not alone.

If you remember just one thing from this chapter, the one key takeaway I want for you is this:

### *All behaviour is communication*

All behaviour is communication, regardless of whether it is good, bad or ugly. And our role as a parent is to understand what our child is attempting to communicate to us; what need is not being met for them and what do they need from us to come back to feeling safe, secure and regulated?

During recent times there has been a paradigm shift amongst current behaviour researchers, with the science focussed on helping us as parents and educators to make the shift from managing behaviours, to using the behaviours as clues to help us, the adults, understand a child's inner reality, support them to be seen and help them *feel felt*.

Unfortunately, there is still the viewpoint amongst many adults and in school settings, that it is a deliberate choice made by kids to act out and wreak havoc on all those in physical proximity. And the only way to manage the behaviour is to issue some form of consequence, such as missing out on fun activities, time outs or suspensions for high levels of challenging behaviour. And as you will recall from a previous chapter, I did impose suspensions, in my role as a Principal, it was a punitive measure used to control a situation and one that I was not always comfortable with.

A quick story from many years ago, where I issued a suspension to a child for being 'continually disobedient', the official reason as per the policy at the time. The suspension was for an accumulation of behaviours, with the last misdemeanour, being the straw that broke the camel's back. The decision to suspend was made following a discussion with his teacher who had been 'putting up' with Mr 11's continual, and intentional poor behaviour. The teacher had had enough. Mr 11's behaviours were seen as him being difficult and naughty and something had to be done about it, hence the suspension.

It was only when I had the pleasure of seeing Mr 11 again who was now Mr 23, in a mutual social setting, that I really understood how punitive measures can impact our kids. After chatting for a while, he respectfully (god love him) raised that suspension with me and his words were:

"You know that suspension you gave me way back when I was in year five, well I didn't do what I was accused of. Someone else did it, but because I was always the naughty kid, the teacher just thought it was me. That suspension hurt me a lot and I still think about it every so often. It was the one time (laughing) I didn't do anything, but still got punished."

His words took the wind out of my sails, and I felt such a sense of shame rise in me that it took my breath away. I processed what he had told me and the only appropriate and warranted response was an apology, which I gave with complete sincerity. I did not know how much of an emotional impact that one consequence had on that young man. And he went on to say at that time that he was struggling at home with some changes within the family and his behaviour was in response to that.

If only I had taken a moment or two, because that's all it takes, to ask, "What is this boy trying to communicate to us?" Instead of going straight to a punitive response.

I will be forever grateful to him for that conversation, as it was the catalyst for my quest as an educator and parent to learn and understand as much as I could about; *behaviour is communication.*

## Regulation: The Key to Taming Big Emotions

I share that story with you only to further illustrate also how adult behaviours and communication can have lasting impacts on kids, without us being cognisant of it.

Whilst I always knew communication was central to relationships, I came to understand on a much deeper level that ALL communication is critical to the parent child relationship. It is the key ingredient to coming to really know, see and feel your child.

But the most powerful piece of knowledge that influenced the way I parented my own, albeit adolescent children by then, as well as other people's children I had in my care, was understanding the brain body connection. Once I understood the brain body connection, I worked really hard to no longer focus on a child's behaviours, but focus on the child, to cultivate the relationship, instead of attempting to solve the problem with punitive responses or with a whole raft of other ineffective strategies.

We will explore the brain body connection a lot more in this chapter with the aim of flipping the thinking from kids being intentionally naughty to recognising that a child's nervous system is being challenged and their little canoe in the river of wellbeing has hit some rapids.

To really understand this paradigm shift, it is important that we bust a couple of myths straight up.

**Myth 1:** Toddlers and little people have tantrums on purpose.

**Myth busted:** Tantrums at any age are a sign that the body's nervous system is feeling unsafe, unseen or in a state of vulnerability or overwhelm. It is a physiological response, not a deliberate or calculated one.

**Myth 2:** Our little humans have full control over their emotions, impulses and behaviours.

**Myth busted:** If you think back to an earlier chapter where I mentioned our brains are not fully developed until the early twenties, then it goes without saying that a child at 2, 3, 4 years of age and beyond, faces an incredibly difficult, if not an impossible task when it comes to regulating their emotions.

The following quote by Mona Delahooke – PhD(2022), a leading researcher into brain body connection, explains it beautifully:

> "… *behaviours provide clues about the state of a child's autonomic nervous system, the unique two - way system of communication between the body and brain. The brain - body connection, our nervous system, serves as a neural platform that influences human behaviours.*" [12]

When I read this quote, I had a huge light bulb moment. It was like a massive flood light had lit up the water and banks of a river of wellbeing for me. I could see the banks of chaos and rigidity clearly enough to know what was coming when a canoe had or was about to crash.

When you can see your child's nervous system is under duress or is vulnerable, you will see behaviours that not only challenge you as a parent but confuse the hell out of you. Think: refusing to put shoes on, throwing a truck when it's time to leave the sandpit, hitting siblings or refusing to walk and wanting to be carried.

On the surface, these responses could be seen as being oppositional, defiant, uncooperative, or just outright rude. But when we take a breath, give it some space and be curious about what is going on right at the very moment, the behaviours actually provide us with clues about what is happening on the inside for the child - this offers an opportunity for a parent to let their child know that they are seen.

Now if this is all sounding a bit 'woo woo', I get it hang in there, be curious and compassionate, because this way of thinking may be challenging your own patterns of interpreting behaviour and ways of responding to challenging behaviour, especially when you are witness to behaviour that makes no sense whatsoever.

It is also a time when we are most likely to be triggered by our kids. I'll talk more about understanding your triggers and the importance of knowing how the body responds in different situations in the next chapter, where we talk about emotional intelligence and how we can tune into our own nervous system responses.

To further understand the inner workings concept, let's look at the Iceberg Theory of which I'm sure many of you are aware of. The Iceberg Theory talks about the observable behaviours that are displayed by children and young people which constitutes the 'tip of the iceberg'. Meanwhile, hidden beneath the water's surface are the emotional triggers that lead to these behaviours. What we see is, as it suggests, is only the tip of the iceberg. There is always way more going on beneath that surface than meets the eye.

*Beyond Bottles Baths and Bed*

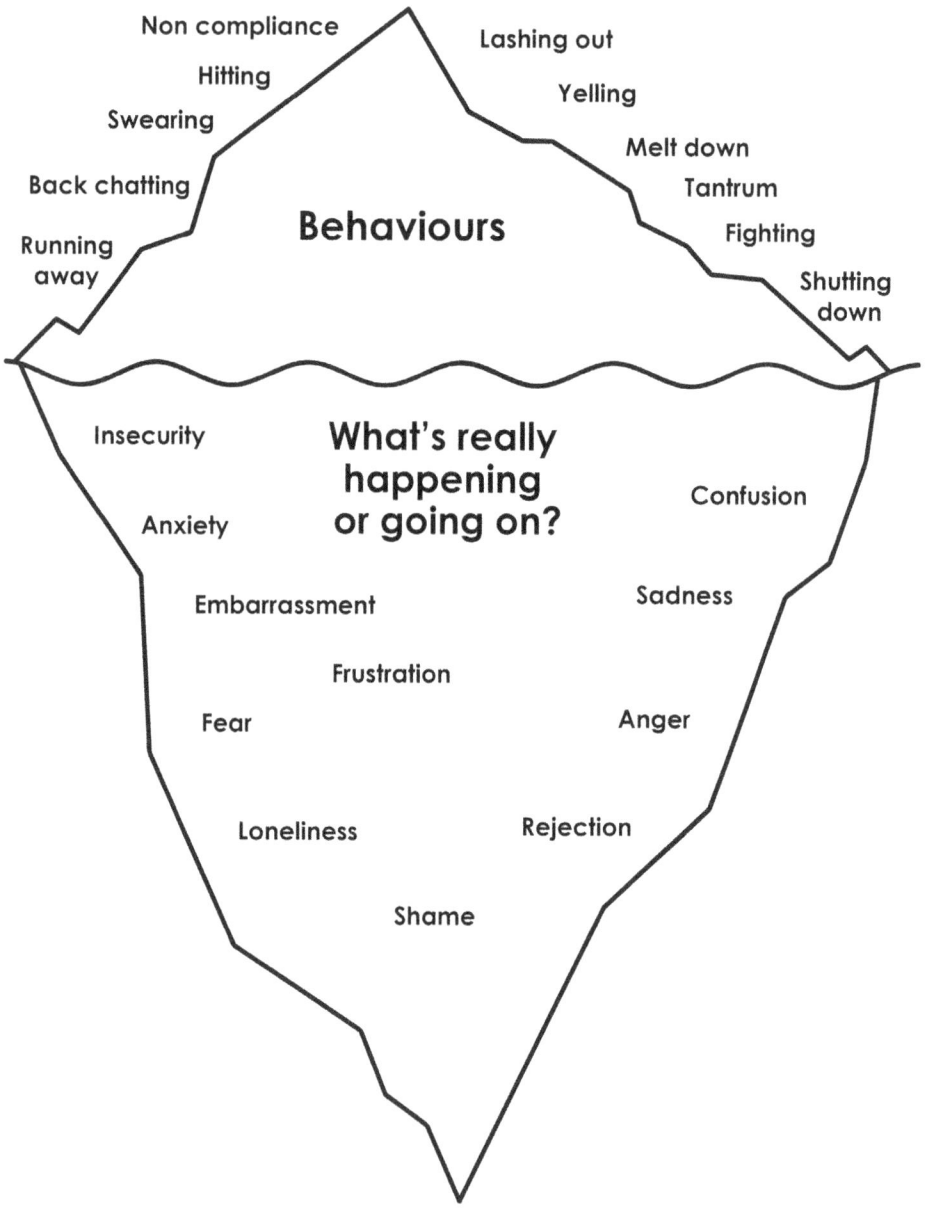

## Regulation: The Key to Taming Big Emotions

Mona Delahooke (2022) - PhD says:

> *"Children rarely act out for no reason or to simply make their parents' lives more challenging (as much as it sometimes feels that way). Our children's behaviours are outward signals of their internal world, indications about that submerged part of the iceberg."* [13]

So instead of trying to eliminate the behaviours we can try our best to understand them as they offer big juicy clues on how our kids experience the world. And underpinning all experiences for both children and adults alike is the quest to feel safe, it is hard wired into core human physiology.

When the body detects a threat to its safety, it can respond in some of the most explosive ways, but also in other ways such as 'withdrawing and checking out', which is just as observable as the externalising responses. The perceived threat to safety can be destabilising for our kids' bodies, and they become dysregulated, aka, smash into the banks of the river of wellbeing.

Dysregulation occurs when their bodies have detected a threat, such as being left out of a game by friends, feeling anxious about meeting new people, or dropping their ice cream on the ground. You get the picture. But lucky for us, we have another tool within easy reach, we can use when our kids become dysregulated.

But before I reveal this powerful tool to you, it's important to firstly understand another critical part of our emotional landscape: self-regulation.

## Self-Regulation – What is it?

Self-regulation is a vital skill that enables us to respond to what life throws at us, in a manner that that is considered and flexible, rather than with sudden emotional outbursts and thoughtless responses.

Perhaps the easiest way to explain regulation is to think of something that activates you or pushes your buttons. It could be a whole range of things; fingers nails on a chalkboard, touching a snake, standing on the edge of a cliff, wet towels on the bathroom floor or that pesky bird singing at 3am.

Now think about how your body is feeling in that moment, what emotion is accompanying those sensations, and what is your initial response? It could be that your heart rate increases as does your breathing. You might have a tight knot in your stomach and all you want to do is run away.

All those feelings, emotions, and sensations is your body attempting to regulate and cope with the current situation and what is happening around you. When we recognise, identify, and respond to our internal physical and emotional states, our body will return more quickly to a calm and relaxed state. This process is called self-regulation.

Self-regulation is the ability to manage our attention and emotions well enough to control impulses, identify emotions, organise thoughts and choosing a coping strategy and sustain attention to monitor your own and other's behaviour, to bring the body back to a state of calm.

 But here's the million dollar question: how do we support our kids to develop these skills? Well, it starts with helping them manage their impulses, teaching them to hit the 'pause button' before reacting and supporting them to learn how to recognise how they are feeling and to trust themselves and their feelings.

And even more exciting and noteworthy about this is, current research tells us that self-regulation lays a foundation for a child's long-term physical, psychological, behavioural, and educational well-being. Kids with strong self-regulation skills do better at school, form better connections with grown-ups and their peers, and they also have fewer issues with their behaviour.

*"We are exquisitely contagious to other people."*
*- Dr Bruce Perry (2020)* [14]

This quote by Dr Bruce Perry, a clinician and researcher in children's mental health and the neurosciences, speaks to the critical role that you play as a parent and the adult in the relationship between yourself and your child.

As adults, it's our ability to remain calm and in control of our emotions that will have the greatest positive impact on a dysregulated child and can affect immediate change in behaviour. Human beings are CONTAGIOUS to the mood and the behaviour and the conditions of those around them and if the dominant contagion is calm, then your child will begin to mirror you.

If you are feeling overwhelmed and your emotions are running high, you are less able to tune into and respond to your overwhelmed child in a way that will help them regain control. In fact, it will lead to even greater dysregulation and disconnection. Remember, your child will mirror your mood and behaviour.

> *"Indeed, the first step in helping a child isn't telling, teaching, or giving instructions. It's being present with the child."*
> Mona Delahooke PHD (2022) [15]

So, what is this powerful tool? It's called Co-regulation.

Co -regulation is simply… a warm, responsive interaction and supportive process between caring adults and babies, children, young people, or other adults. It is a contagiously calm and emotionally intelligent adult helping to regain control over another's dysregulated nervous system.

Through co-regulation we can help our children learn to manage their emotions and behaviours through loving interactions with them, our relationships.

By co-regulating, we create a safe space where children feel secure and learn to make sense of their feelings and the sensations in their body.

Researchers Rosanbalm & Murray (2017) state:

> *"There are three broad categories of support that caregivers can provide to young children to help them develop the foundational self-regulatory skills that they will need to get the best start in life".* [16]

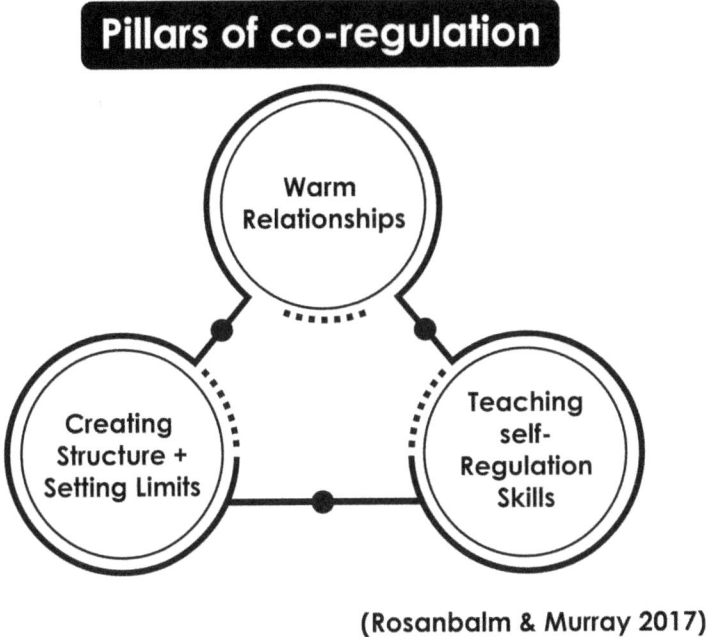

(Rosanbalm & Murray 2017)

As you can see in the diagram, whilst each of the categories covers specific aspects of co- regulation, there is a very clear relationship between each, when all three are in place, they come together to provide the foundation for emotional development success.

Let's take a closer look at each of the categories and what they mean in practice:

**Warm Relationships:**

- Show love and affection.
- Pay attention and respond to what your child needs and wants.
- Be there for support during times of stress.
- Take an interest in them and what they care about.

- Treat with respect and value their individuality.
- Be committed to being there and caring, no matter what.

## Creating Structure & Setting Limits:

- Create an environment that is safe and makes your child feel emotionally secure.
- Encourage exploring and learning that matches their age and abilities.
- Protect them from things that can cause stress or harm.
- Follow regular routines and have clear expectations.
- Implement well-defined logical consequences for negative behaviours.
- Promote a sense of security.

## Teaching Self-Regulation Skills

- Show and teach how to control emotions and behaviour.
- Provide opportunities to practice self-regulation skills.
- Encourage using those skills with reminders and cues.
- Acknowledge and reward progress in using the skills.
- Give support when they need help with self-regulation.
- Be like a coach, guiding and supporting the development of self-regulation skills.

So now you know what co-regulation is and to dispel any concerns or worry, let's talk briefly about what it is not:

## CO REGULATION IS NOT …

Just another way of spoiling or coddling your child, coddling and co-regulating are very different. One is incessantly indulging your child, never saying no, whilst the other is attending to your child's physical and emotional needs.

Co-regulating does not mean that we make sure our children are always happy and shielding them from life's challenges. Meeting a child's needs for safety and security doesn't mean giving them everything they want or not letting them struggle with difficult emotions. And it certainly doesn't mean we need to sit in close physical proximity and wait it out while they are riding the waves of big emotions.

As a parent, you can compassionately observe your child's struggle and also set firm and appropriate boundaries to ensure their safety by offering just enough support so they stay within the challenge zone, which enables them to grow emotionally in a safe and supported way.

The process of learning to self-regulate is long and complex, but researchers in this particular field have found, time after time, that co-regulation is the superpower that supports our kids' capacity to learn to self-regulate.

Co regulation is about building love and trust in the relationship, so that the child knows we will consistently show up for them and help them when they encounter struggle or upset, and that we will bring our calmness to help them regain control.

Co-regulation is NOT about letting your kid rule the roost and behave however they want, whenever they want, kids NEED boundaries. Kids need boundaries to feel safe and understand how to navigate the world. It gives them a clear picture of what's okay and what's not, as long as we are clear that we are saying no to a particular behaviour, not the emotion associated with that behaviour.

For example: your 4-year-old hits you. An automatic response could be to respond by getting angry, grabbing Miss 4 and marching her off to her room, whilst saying through clenched teeth, 'hitting is not ok'.

Whilst this is not the world's worst parenting response, this chapter is to about taking a moment, be curious and asking what's going on. Why did my child behave that way? What do I need to teach? How can I teach it?

The hit could have been a response due to your child being told to wait until you finished folding some washing before you would be able to play with them. So, the hit may have been to gain your attention. Was it a desirable way to get it? No. Was it developmentally appropriate? Yes, as Miss 4 is still learning to self-regulate and she is not yet old enough to self-calm or act quickly enough to prevent lashing out.

Rather than working on autopilot and being reactive, a response could be along the lines of the following:

Pull her close and let her know you're all ears. Then, you could say something like,

"Seems like waiting is tough. You really want us to play, and you're mad that I am folding washing. Is that how you're feeling?"

She might just fire back with a grumpy, "Yeah!"

But that's okay because she'll see that you're there for her and you have her attention.

This is the perfect time to chat. As she'll more than likely settle and tune in, which provides you with the opportunity to make eye contact, explain that hitting isn't cool, and talk about what else she could have done —like using her words when she's annoyed.

It is not always easy to respond in a calm non-reactive way, we are all human and we are going to react on autopilot. It takes time and practice to build in the pause for ourselves and get curious before responding. But the more aware we are, the more automatic it will become, so in the meantime have compassion and repair. Repair a rupture if your response feels horrible for you or your child. Repairing the rupture quickly, will ensure your child knows they are seen, heard, felt, valued and loved unconditionally.

In conclusion, I hope the super power of coregulation is a tool that you already utilise from your tool kit, but if the concept is unfamiliar to you, I encourage you to try and be mindful of your reactions when things get a bit wobbly. Awareness will empower you to share your sense of calm, which will positively impact those around you.

To finish this chapter, I'd like to share with you another quote from the amazing Mona Delahooke PhD(2022):

"When we co regulate or share connection with our children over time, the experiences form memories of feeling safe with another and our children grow up expecting that others will meet their needs. When you give your child loving experiences of connection, you are giving them the best possible head start in facing life's challenges." [17]

# Chapter 6

# Happiness Unleashed: The Hidden Power of Emotional Intelligence

*"Between stimulus and response there is a space. In that space is our power to choose our response. In our response lies our growth and our freedom." – Viktor Frankl*

We've covered a lot of ground so far and almost all of it has been focused on the parent and child connection, and the brain body connection, to support the development of our kids emotional landscape.

For this chapter, I want to take a step back and spend a little time talking about the critical role emotional intelligence plays in the parenting journey, but also in our lives in general.

The Oxford Dictionary definition of emotional intelligence as:

> *"The capacity to be aware of, control, and express one's emotions, and to handle interpersonal relationships judiciously and empathetically."*
>
> *"Emotional intelligence is the key to both personal and professional success."* [18]

The first line in the definition sums up neatly and concisely what we have just been talking about in the previous chapter: our ability to manage our emotions when our kids need us the most. There is no better moment than the present to engage in a little self-reflection in the context of the definition and think about how it influences how we are, and how we choose to be with our kids.

Emotional intelligence, or EQ, as it is also known, is the ability to communicate effectively and build strong connections and relationships. And if we think outside of our relationships with our kids for a moment and reflect on some of our work or other family relationships, I'm sure you will identify people in your life that do not have good EQ skills.

It's those people in our lives who; are blunt and in your face, send whiney or passive aggressive emails, are completely hopeless at reading the room or talk incessantly about themselves. I think we all know them, and possibly some of us are them, but not likely given you are reading this book.

People with low EQ skills are the ones we would prefer to avoid, even to the extent of crossing the road and walking on the opposite footpath, just to avoid them. Why? Because people with low EQ lack self-awareness, possess a limited ability to be empathetic and understanding of others, oh and best of all they love to blame. And funnily enough it's all of these attributes that grind the gears of a person who has good or well developed EQ skills.

Let's check out what Emotional Intelligence look like at a glance:

| Signs of High Emotional Intelligence | Signs of Low Emotional Intelligence |
| --- | --- |
| Good listener | Not listening |
| Cooperative | Being argumentative |
| Taking responsibility | Blaming others |
| Calm composure | Emotional outbursts |
| Effective coping | Poor coping skills |
| Strong sense of self awareness | Behaves insensitively |
| Shows empathy for others | Oblivious to the feelings of others |
| Curious and eager to learn | Have to be right |
| Shows interest in others | Turns the conversation towards themselves |
| Gets along well with others | Struggle with relationships |

As you read the table above, I am guessing you can see a very clear link to the themes and topics we have covered so far. There is an opportunity here to reflect on your EQ skills, without judgment and with compassion, because if we want to raise happy emotionally connected kids, then as parents, it is critical that we look inwards first.

If your EQ skills are not great, then it is really challenging for your kids to learn the skills, because as we know, humans are contagious to the mood, the behaviour and the conditions of those around them. We need to support our kids to learn the skills, not just expect it of them and modelling is the most powerful teaching tool ever.

Next time you are playing or just being with your child, especially little ones, note how they watch you closely and mimic what you do. They are taking it all in and learning about the world and being in it, just by observing you.

For example, if we smash into the banks of the river of wellbeing (we all do, it isn't just a space for kids), and we respond by ranting and raving and blaming others, then we are modelling to our kids that's the way to manage the situation when things don't go how we want or thought they should. When we can effectively regulate our emotions, we are demonstrating how to manage stress, frustration, and sadness in healthy ways, thereby teaching our kids the invaluable skills for emotional self-regulation.

Parents who use observation and self-awareness tend to manage challenges without resorting to outbursts or unhealthy behaviours and by doing so, show their kids how to respond to their emotions constructively if they come up against challenging or difficult situations.

In the context of parenting, emotional intelligence holds profound significance as it shapes how we interact with our kids, it fosters healthy family dynamics, and lays the foundation for a child's emotional development and overall well-being.

You are probably thinking, that's all well and good, I understand what high and low EQ looks like and how important it is to help our kids to grow into happy and emotionally connected kids. But now what?

Start with looking inwards and by looking inwards, I mean really becoming aware of what is happening for you, that is; having self-awareness.

Self-awareness is the foundational component of emotional intelligence. It is the crucial aspect of understanding and managing our own emotions, as well as those of others. And is defined as the ability to recognise and comprehend one's own emotions, thoughts, and behaviours and their impact on oneself and others.

The bottom line is, if we want to raise happy, self-aware kids who are emotionally intelligent, then we need to be self-aware and emotionally intelligent ourselves.

So, my invitation to you is to take a moment and reflect on your day and jot down or keep a mental note of the emotions that you have experienced so far today. It might feel a little weird to start with, but the goal here is to tune in (as we do for our kids) to your emotional landscape and acknowledge the emotions that have shown up for you today. It's a nice gentle way to tap into your self-awareness and notice those subtle shifts in your emotional state.

I'll start, as it may help as you think through your day.

My day started with a very early alarm, and I woke from a deep sleep, so when that alarm went off I was a bit **annoyed.** I dragged myself out of bed, still feeling **tired** from a night of broken sleep. I boiled the kettle, but forgot to top it up with water so, when I poured myself a cup of tea there was less than half a cup of hot water and that **frustrated** me no end.

Later, I logged on for my first meeting for the day and **happily** chatted to my colleagues online. All was going well until the chairperson announced I was next on the agenda, and I had 15 minutes to deliver my presentation. Umm, wait, what?? A rush of **surprise** flooded through me as no one had told me I had been included on the agenda and that I was to present at that meeting. I was left feeling totally **embarrassed** in front 25 of my closest (wink) work colleagues and had to politely apologise and maintain some form of composure. I sat there with my camera still on, filled with **shame,** as I imagined people were thinking how unprepared and how terrible I was at my job. When that meeting finish, man, I was **angry.** I was on the hunt to find out who composed the agenda….

All those emotions and it was only 9.30am! So, you get the picture. There are multiple times throughout the day where we are experiencing a raft of emotions, but most of the time we don't take a moment to reflect on our emotional state.

The more we reflect, the better we can see where we need to be a bit more mindful or where we are absolutely killing it! It could be that you are tuned in and patient when your child is yelling at you for ice cream, but struggle to remain calm when they are completely dysregulated in a noisy and busy environment.

Through regular self-reflection you will start to recognise where your blind spots are and learn to address them, so that you show up for your kids in a way that makes them feel seen, safe, soothed, and secure. Remembering all the while that there is no such thing as perfect parenting, you are going to mess it up and miscue sometimes and that's ok! As long as there is repair as soon as possible, all will be well.

It's during the self-reflection time you also come to understand what your parenting style is. You'll recall in chapter one I shared with you a whole range of parenting styles, including: Authoritarian, Authoritative, Permissive, Uninvolved/ Neglectful and so on.

As you ponder which parenting style you predominantly are, it is also interesting to note where your preferred parenting style came from. Without a doubt, our parenting style comes from the way we were parented, but with a few little tweaks. Because I'm pretty certain that there are some things from our childhood that we decided not to run with in our own parenting journey for whatever reason. But let me just call out, that is not a judgment of how you or I for that matter, were parented. Parents do their best with what they know at the point in time - remember, all parents want the best for their kids, period.

Let's look at a few familiar parenting styles through the lens of emotional intelligence and as we continue on the conversation about EQ and parenting styles. Keep in mind that we are thinking about how parents deal with their kids' emotions, not the child overall.

## *Permissive parenting*

Parents with a permissive style are usually warm and responsive, but are lenient and indulgent, allowing their kids to have a great deal of freedom and autonomy with few rules or boundaries. Without boundaries, kids may encounter challenges in school and social situations where rules and structure are more prevalent. Paradoxically, kids raised with too much freedom and a lack of structure may experience insecurity and anxiety. The absence of clear boundaries can make them feel unsafe or unsure of their place in the world. It's also interesting to note some parents may choose permissive parenting as a reaction to their own experiences with strict or authoritarian parenting styles. They may want to avoid the potential negative impacts of overly controlling or punitive parenting.

## *Dismissive parenting*

A dismissive parenting style is when parents are uninvolved and unresponsive (avoidant attachment pattern) to their child's needs. This type of parenting is often characterised by an indifference toward their child's feelings, behaviours, and problems. Parents may be dismissive by ignoring their child's emotions, dismissing their child's concerns, and or disregarding their child's requests. They might say things like:

- You're too sensitive.
- Why even bother trying.
- You'll never be as good as your brother.

This type of parenting can damage a child's self-esteem and can lead to feelings of worthlessness, anger, and resentment.

## *Unconscious and Unaware parenting*

Unconscious parenting is when a parent is unaware of their own beliefs, attitudes, and values (ambivalent attachment pattern) and how it impacts their parenting. Unconscious parenting is often rooted in the parent's past experiences and is perpetuated by the parent's own lack of awareness and understanding of how their behaviour and attitudes are affecting their parenting. Unconscious parenting can be seen in a variety of situations, such as a parent's lack of understanding of their own emotional needs and how it affects their parenting, or a parent's inability to recognize their own biases.

Unaware parenting is when a parent is unaware of their child's needs and how their parenting is impacting the child's development. It can be seen in situations such as a parent not being able to recognise the child's emotional needs or developmental needs, not understanding the impact of their behaviour on the child, or not providing the emotional support that the child needs. Unaware parenting is often rooted in a lack of knowledge, or understanding, and can lead to the child feeling neglected and unimportant.

It might look and sound like:

- You'll be ok in a while. Shrug it off.
- It's not important for you to know why.
- I'm the adult here, so I know best.

## Compassionate and Conscious parenting

Compassionate and conscious parenting (secure attachment pattern) is a style of parenting that emphasises empathy, understanding, and communication. This style of parenting focuses on understanding a child's feelings and needs and providing them with the support and guidance they need to thrive. Compassionate and conscious parenting is based on the idea that children are complex individuals who have their own thoughts, feelings, and needs. It encourages parents to cultivate an environment of love, respect, and open communication in which children have the freedom to express themselves and their feelings.

It also encourages parents to be aware of their own emotions and how they affect their children. This style of parenting requires that parents are mindful of their own needs and emotions, while also being mindful of their child's needs. It emphasises the importance of understanding and responding to a child's emotions in a non-judgmental and supportive way. Compassionate and conscious parenting is about creating a secure and safe environment where children can explore and grow in their own unique ways.

What it might look like and sound like:

- It's ok to make mistakes that is how we learn
- I can see you are upset, can you tell me what's bothering you?

It's quite clear from these examples which of the parenting styles is most conducive to helping our kids grow into emotionally intelligent people, so it is helpful to know which parenting style we are most aligned to and where our areas for growth and learning lie.

The next step in teaching our kids about emotional intelligence is to take a moment to reflect on ourselves and figure out what triggers us. Now, if you think you don't have any triggers, may I be so bold as to say you are either a saint or in denial, because we all have them. Some are quite significant responses, while others have less of an impact.

What triggers you? To develop our EQ skills, we need to manage our triggers and be aware of what things your kids or other people in your life do that pushes your buttons.

Being triggered can result from several things, including:

**Unmet Expectations:** when our kids don't meet our expectations or behave in ways we didn't anticipate, it can be frustrating and trigger negative emotions.

**Stress and Fatigue:** parents often have a lot on their plates, from work responsibilities to household chores and childcare. Stress and exhaustion can lower your patience threshold and make you more prone to being triggered by your kids' behaviour.

**Past Trauma or Triggers:** your own childhood experiences, unresolved trauma, or past triggers can resurface when dealing with your children. Certain behaviours or situations might remind you of your own difficult experiences, leading to heightened emotional reactions.

**Lack of Control:** children can be unpredictable, and parents may feel a lack of control over their children's actions and decisions. This lack of control can lead to frustration and trigger negative emotions.

**Developmental Stages:** children go through various developmental stages, and each stage comes with its own challenges.

**Personal Triggers:** personal issues, insecurities, or unresolved emotions can surface when interacting with your children. Your kids might unintentionally press your emotional buttons, leading to a reaction that seems disproportionate to the situation.

**Communication Issues:** difficulty in effective communication with your children can lead to frustration and feeling triggered. If you're not able to express your thoughts and feelings or if your child isn't listening, it can escalate emotions.

**Lack of Self-Care:** neglecting self-care can make you more susceptible to being triggered. When you're physically or emotionally drained, it's harder to manage your reactions to your children's behaviour.

**Cultural and Societal Pressures:** societal expectations and cultural norms about parenting can also play a role. Parents may feel pressured to conform to certain standards, which can lead to feelings of inadequacy and frustration if they believe they are falling short.

Here are some more common triggers and responses from parents:

| Common Triggers | Common Responses |
| --- | --- |
| Back chatting | Shouting |
| Sibling fighting | Smacking |
| Arguing | Time outs |
| Whining | Walking away |
| Ignoring requests | Threats |
| Being disrespectful | Giving in |
| Leaving a trail of clothes and toys | Ignoring the behaviour |

Now we've outlined some triggers and responses. The key is to align an emotion to it, in other words, identify how do our triggers make us feel?

Think about how you feel when your kid back chats you and refuses to eat his dinner. A possible response could be to shout at him to eat his dinner or threaten with 'no dessert', but what that often leads to is more dysregulation, anger and noncompliance, which leads to you feeling more and more angry and frustrated. Doesn't sound like fun, does it?

But rather than just saying I feel angry, I encourage you to think about all the emotions we experience. We have access to words such as agitated, hurt, annoyed, tired, frustrated and so many more. It is at this step where we 'name it to tame it'.

I'm sure the majority of you would be familiar with that phrase coined by Dr Dan Seigel (2010), where he talks about naming and identifying your emotions because:

> *"When you experience significant internal stress and anxiety, you can reduce stress by up to 50% by simply noticing and naming your state. If we can see the emotion, we do not have to be the emotion."* (19)

Now this is not just some random statistic that Dr Dan Seigel has plucked out of thin air. It is backed by scientific evidence and a 50% reduction in stress just by naming it, is awesome!

If we can learn to manage our triggers by using strategies such as naming it to tame it, we will not only become more emotionally intelligent in our parenting, but we have the bonus of modelling the strategy to our children. By taking a moment to pause, identify the emotion, and understand its source, we can gain better control over our responses and make more thoughtful decisions.

Emotional intelligence is not only beneficial, but essential for parents. It transforms parenting from a job to an opportunity for personal growth, developing meaningful connections, and nurturing emotional development in our kids.

Parents who cultivate their own emotional intelligence contribute to a positive family environment where communication, understanding, and empathy thrive. By modelling emotional intelligence, you are setting your child on a path toward emotional well-being, resilience, and success in their future relationships and life adventures.

> *See you over the page where we will talk about how to really super charge and support your EQ skills, through self-care.*

# Chapter 7

# Caring for the Caretaker: Embracing Looking After You

*"I have just three things to teach: simplicity, patience, compassion. These three are your greatest treasures." – Lao Tzu*

Even under the best of circumstances, parenting can be exhausting and challenging. When we become parents, our lives change immediately and we become intertwined with the well-being of our children, and their happiness and growth becomes our top priority. And amongst all the responsibilities and demands of parenting, it becomes way too easy to overlook our own needs and neglect self-care.

When we reflect on what we've learned about co-regulation and emotional intelligence, it's pretty easy to see the most critical element in it all, is YOU. It's how you show up in the moment and it is reflected in how you hold your body, tone of voice, the words you use, facial expressions and your gestures.

Mona Delahooke PhD(2022) says:

> *"As important as it is to co regulate with our children, we need to be okay ourselves. That doesn't mean we have to feel our best all the time, but rather we have to feel okay enough to share time with our children in the green pathway - where the really "good stuff" happens: the snuggles, the giggles, the moments of tenderness and comfort, or sturdiness, when our child needs it."* [20]

So, in this chapter, I want to focus on you and talk about self-care as not being a selfish act, but a crucial part of how you show up for your child.

With compassion and without judgment, we'll look at different ways to improve the odds of being able to show up as our most regulated selves, on most occasions. Because remember, good enough parenting is good enough!.

When I think back to times when I was a young mum, there are responses to moments that I wish I could undo, because they still make me feel uncomfortable when I think about them.

One time in particular sticks with me. I had returned to full-time work and had to be out of the house by 7am sharp every day. In amongst trying to get myself dressed and getting food packed for lunches, I had two little people who needed to have breakfast and to put their clothes, socks and shoes on. I remember, almost running from one thing to another, all the while watching the clock and prompting the kids to get dressed and find their shoes and socks.

## Caring for the Caretaker: Embracing Looking After You

We'd done this routine so many mornings before, but this morning I just lost my sh!t.

The kids were having a great time, rolling around play fighting on the floor in the lounge room, still in their pyjamas, completely oblivious to my repeated requests to: "Put your clothes on. Find your shoes and socks. Find your backpacks. Stop playing and get dressed." And on and on it went, without any movement from the kids, except to continue their game of play fighting.

I just exploded! All my frustration and anger came spewing out of my mouth. I shouted (which was totally out of character for me) at them to stop. My shout didn't get their attention initially so, I repeated the request to stop again, but this time, I was so angry, I had my whole body involved, I was yelling and waving my arms around. It got their attention alright, but what stays with me is the look on their faces. It was a complete shock. It was as if they were seeing and hearing me for the first time. Their little faces and bodies told the whole story. They were not only shocked but appeared to pull back and draw a little closer to each other, as if looking for safety.

But no, I wasn't done there. I yelled at them again to go to their rooms and do as I had asked. They both jumped up and moved silently to their rooms. I was left standing there with what can only be described as a huge amount of shame replacing the anger that was there less than 5 seconds ago. Talk about going from 0 to 100 in a split second. Definitely not one of my finest parenting moments!

And just so you know we got out of the house by 7am, but it was a very quiet car ride to before school care, and unfortunately back then I did not know the power of repair when there was a rupture, hence I did not apologise. I know my poor babies suffered that day because of the way I showed up for them, but not in a way I am proud of because for a fleeting moment, I was their source of fear.

When I look back at the time, there was a bit going on. I held very high expectations for myself in both my personal and professional life. I thought I had to be a super mum and could do it all. But in fact, I let a 'clock' in this instance, be a cause for dysregulation and stress. A bloody clock! My brain was so focussed on 7am, I did not check in with myself when I noticed my body reacting to the stress of potentially leaving home after 7am, which would throw out the rest of the day.

But I also realised that it wasn't just about the clock, it was because I was tired, felt pulled from pillar to post, unconsciously worried that I wasn't being a good parent and that my kids weren't eating enough veggies, and god forbid that I arrive at work five minutes later than usual!

But I have some compassion and have reconciled with myself that, whilst it wasn't one of my finest parenting moments, I was just trying to do my best at the time.

Which brings me once again to the purpose of this chapter – looking after you – mum or dad. Now this might be a chapter that you are really tempted to skip, but can I encourage you to start the journey of investing in your self-care (if you don't already), by hanging in there and reading some of the suggestions in the coming pages. And just to reassure you this is not a guilt trip about not going to the gym regularly or blowing off a yoga session at the beach, it's about thinking a little differently and prioritising you, so you can be fully present and tune into your child.

Let's jump in:

## *Self-Care and Compassion*

In a recent study conducted by Parenting Research Centre in Victoria(2022), called the Parenting Today in Victoria study, they identified a number of factors associated with parents' practice of self-care. Key findings of the study included:

> *"A considerable proportion of parents – almost a quarter – did not regularly practice self-care."*

> *"Better physical and mental health among parents was associated with greater self-care, and poorer physical and mental health were associated with lower self-compassion."*

> *"Parents who practiced self-care were more confident in their parenting role than parents who did not practice self-care."* [21]

Practicing self-care and compassion is a key ingredient to feeling more confident as a parent and the positive spin off of that is, greater connections and bonds with our kids.

It's also interesting to note the **Zero -3 Early Connections Last a Lifetime Centre** reports:

> *"Our Tuning In survey showed that nearly 9 in 10 parents across the board feel judged (90% mums and 85% dads), and almost half say they feel judged all the time or nearly all the time (46% mums; 45% dads)."* [22]

So, if you are feeling judged or you are being self-critical, you are definitely not alone. As those stats clearly demonstrate.

It's tough out there, but if you are currently in the mindset that self-compassion is nice to do or have but is unnecessary, I encourage you to continue reading.

Dr Kirstin Neff is an associate professor at the University of Texas in Austin's department of educational psychology, and she has done some incredible research on the topic of self-compassion. She describes self-compassion as treating oneself with the same kindness and understanding that you would offer to a close friend during times of struggle or setbacks. By doing so we are utilising a potent resource for coping and resilience, leading to significant enhancement in both our mental and physical well-being. And what that means is; if we nurture our brains and bodies we will be more likely to show up for kids in a regulated way.

So how do we practice self-compassion?

There are a myriad of things we can do but, I am going to touch on just a few here to spark your thoughts about some self-care activities that feel right for you.

In the first instance, I'm going to lean on Dr Mona Delahooke's (2022) research backed exercise to simply sense and acknowledge a challenge, recognising that we are not alone in those challenges and then offering ourselves some kindness, just as would do for your kids if they were having a hard time.

Dr Delahooke's(2022) self-compassion break is another tool that can be added to your tool kit and is accessible at any point in time. It goes like this:

### Practice: The Self - Compassion Break

1. Notice and acknowledge a difficult moment, situation or problem and say to yourself, "This is hard" or "This is stressful" or even simply "Ouch."
2. Remind yourself that you are not alone in suffering and acknowledge or say to yourself "I'm not alone" or "This is how it feels when people are struggling this way" or "All parents suffer at times."
2. Offer yourself kindness in some way, such as saying silently, "May I be kind or gentle to myself" or "May I give myself what I need" or even asking "What do I need in this moment?" [23]

These 3 simple gestures will bring you into the moment and reassure your nervous system that you are safe and ok.

*"Supporting our own sense of compassion and wellbeing makes us better equipped to do the same for our children."* [24]

## *Sleep*

Let's face it: when you become a parent, your sleep patterns get thrown into a blender. The early days with a newborn are a whirlwind of nappy changes, feeding sessions, and trying to soothe a crying baby. Forget about those eight hours of uninterrupted sleep you used to love and cherish. Suddenly, even a few hours of shut eye will feel like a luxury.

Sleep deprivation and parenting - it's a combo that often feels like an initiation into a secret society. Whether you're a first-time parent or a seasoned pro, the struggle with sleep is all too real. But, beyond the jokes about being a 'mombie' or 'zombie dad' it's essential to understand how sleep deprivation may impact your parenting journey.

Let's break it down. Sleep deprivation is essentially a fancy way of saying you're not getting enough sleep. In the parenting realm, this usually happens because a baby or toddler has an uncanny knack for waking up at the least convenient times. Those glorious eight-hour nights of uninterrupted slumber, become a distant memory. In fact, it's during this time parents more than likely fantasise about a few consecutive hours of shut-eye.

So, what's the big deal with sleep deprivation, and how does it impact parenting? Well, it's not just about feeling tired; it's about the whole shebang – body, mind, and emotions.

Physically, it's like your body's defence system goes on holiday. Physical symptoms of sleep deprivation may include:

- **Fatigue and Sleepiness** - the most apparent physical symptom of sleep deprivation is feeling extremely tired and sleepy during the day. This overwhelming sense of exhaustion can make it challenging to stay awake and alert.
- **Impaired Coordination and Balance** - you may find it more challenging to undertake tasks that require fine motor skills, such as typing, using tools, or even driving.
- **Muscle Aches and Weakness** - you may experience muscle stiffness, tension, or even muscle twitches. Chronic sleep deprivation can contribute to long-term muscle pain.
- **Increased Appetite and Weight Gain** - disrupt the balance of hormones that regulate appetite, leading to increased hunger and cravings for unhealthy, calorie-dense foods. This can cause weight gain over time, as sleep-deprived individuals are more likely to consume excess calories.
- **Hormonal Imbalances** - alter the balance of hormones in your body, including stress hormones like cortisol. This can cause hormonal imbalances that affect various bodily functions, from mood regulation to metabolism.

Mentally and emotionally, it's like your brain's on a perpetual rollercoaster. Remember those times when you could effortlessly juggle multiple tasks and solve complex problems? Say goodbye to that superhero version of yourself. You're now the main character in a saga of lost keys, forgotten grocery lists and mood swings. It may also look like:

- **Mood Swings**: sleep-deprived individuals often experience rapid and extreme mood swings. You might go from feeling irritable and short-tempered one moment to being overly emotional or tearful the next.
- **Irritability and Agitation**: lack of sleep can leave you feeling easily irritated, agitated, or frustrated over minor inconveniences. Everyday annoyances that you might usually brush off can become sources of intense irritation when you are sleep deprived.
- **Increased Emotional Sensitivity**: sleep deprivation can heighten emotional sensitivity, making you more prone to emotional reactions. You may feel more emotionally fragile or experience intense emotional responses to situations that would typically not affect you as strongly.
- **Social Withdrawal**: due to the emotional toll of sleep deprivation, individuals may withdraw from social activities and isolate themselves, which can further impact mental health and lead to feelings of loneliness.

So not only does sleep deprivation impact on a personal level, but it can also impair your ability to respond to your child's needs effectively. It can impede your ability to provide the emotional support and nurturing that your child needs for a healthy emotional connection that builds secure attachment.

Over time, chronic sleep deprivation in parents can have a negative impact on a child's emotional well-being and behaviour. When you're running on empty, it's tough to be patient and attentive to your kids. Small problems become epic crisis, and you might find yourself yelling over spilled milk (literally) meaning the quality of the moments with your kids could take a hit.

*Caring for the Caretaker: Embracing Looking After You*

So, what's the suggested game plan for a sleep-deprived parent?

- **Establish a consistent sleep schedule**: try to stick to a regular sleep schedule as much as possible, even on weekends. This can help regulate your body's internal clock and improve the quality of your sleep.
- **Prioritise naps:** if you have the opportunity, take short power naps during the day when your child is sleeping or occupied. Even a 20–30-minute nap can provide a quick energy boost.
- **Share nighttime responsibilities**: if you have a partner, take turns getting up at night to care for your child. This can allow both of you to get more uninterrupted sleep.
- **Sleep when your baby sleeps:** newborns tend to sleep a lot during the day. Use this time to rest and nap, rather than trying to catch up on chores or work.
- **Limit screen time before bed:** reduce exposure to screens (phones, tablets, TV) before bedtime, as the blue light can interfere with your ability to fall asleep. Instead, engage in relaxing activities like reading or taking a warm bath.
- **Manage stress:** parenthood can be stressful, and stress can worsen sleep problems. Practice stress-reduction techniques, such as deep breathing exercises, mindfulness, or yoga, to help you relax.
- **Limit caffeine and alcohol:** both caffeine and alcohol can disrupt sleep patterns. Try to limit their consumption, especially in the hours leading up to bedtime.
- **Stay hydrated and eat well:** proper hydration and a balanced diet can help with overall energy levels.
- **Seek help and support:** support systems are your lifelines. Call in reinforcements. Let grandparents or your

trusted best friend swoop in for a few hours of babysitting so you can rejuvenate. Trust me, I can guarantee most grandparents can't wait to help, so reach out.
- **Talk to a healthcare professional:** if sleep deprivation becomes chronic and significantly impacts your daily functioning, consider speaking with a healthcare provider. They can offer guidance and may suggest sleep aids or other treatments.

But most importantly, cut yourself some slack. Parenting is a marathon, not a sprint, and sleep deprivation is just one of the hurdles. Your kids will grow up faster than you can imagine, and someday, you'll look back on these sleepless nights with a mix of nostalgia and amazement.

## *Mindful Breathing - the superpower for restoring calm*

Mindful breathing offers a multitude of invaluable benefits for parents navigating the demands of raising children in today's fast-paced world. In the midst of the chaos and responsibilities, taking a few moments each day to practice mindful breathing can be transformative.

First and foremost, mindful breathing can provide you with a tool to manage stress. It's accessible, and it just requires an awareness of your breath and doesn't need any planning or extra time to do. Mindful breathing provides you with a moment to step back, take a breath, and regain your composure in the face of challenges.

*Caring for the Caretaker: Embracing Looking After You*

Benefits of mindful breathing include:

- **Stress reduction:** when you engage in mindful breathing techniques, you activate your body's relaxation response, which lowers cortisol levels and promotes a sense of calm.
- **Improved emotional regulation**: mindful breathing helps you become more aware of your emotions and how they manifest in your body. This heightened awareness allows you to respond to challenging situations with greater emotional control and resilience, reducing impulsive reactions, and promoting healthier relationships.
- **Enhanced focus and concentration:** practicing mindful breathing sharpens your ability to concentrate and stay focused on the present moment. By training your mind to stay in the here and now, you can boost productivity, make better decisions, and perform tasks more efficiently.
- **Better physical health:** having positive effects on your physical health. It can lower blood pressure, reduce the risk of heart disease, and improve lung function.

Here's a quick how to, to get you started:

**Step 1. Inhale slowly:** take a slow and deep breath in through your nose. Count to four as you inhale, making sure it's a gentle and relaxed breath.

**Step 2. Exhale slowly:** now exhale the breath slowly and steadily through your mouth or nose. Again, count to four as you breathe out.

**Step 3. Repeat:** continue this pattern of inhaling for a count of four and exhaling for a count of four. You can adjust the count to a pace that feels comfortable for you; the key is to keep it slow and steady.

**Step 4. Stay relaxed:** as you practice slow breathing, focus on keeping your body and mind relaxed. You may find it helpful to close your eyes and imagine tension leaving your body with each exhale.

**Step 5. Practice regularly:** you can do slow breathing for a few minutes whenever you need to relax, reduce anxiety, or calm your mind.

Mindful breathing has many benefits and is available to us at every moment and if you combine this with the compassion practice mentioned earlier, you have a super charged self-care tool right at your fingertips, or lungs in this case!

And the final tip I want to share with you is the wise words from Mona Delahooke PhD(2022), and is a resilience building tip:

> *"The most important tool in our parenting toolkit is our own emotional and physical wellbeing, but that doesn't mean we have to be perfect; the key is developing awareness to identify your needs, finding self-care strategies that work for you and having compassion for yourself to do so. Valuing your own mental health and the ability to feel emotionally stable is one of the best things you can do for yourself and your child."* [25]

If you are reading this sentence, thank you for hanging in there and not skipping this chapter. You have given yourself the gift of investing in your self-care and my hope for you is that you may try one or two of the suggestions, when things feel a little

*Caring for the Caretaker: Embracing Looking After You*

rough or even just to show yourself a little kindness. But either way, just know you are doing a great job and it is not at all selfish to take a moment and focus on your wellbeing and emotional landscape. In fact, it is critical.

*"Taking care of yourself is part of taking care of your kids"*
*- Lenny Lemons*

# Chapter 8

# One-of-a-Kind: Recognising the Beauty of Our Uniqueness

*"Every child is gifted. They just unwrap their packages at different times." - Unknown*

It almost goes without saying that in a book such as this one, focussed on emotional connection and having a sense of belonging, that the statement 'we are all unique', must be included. Why? Because it is the absolute truth, there is no one anywhere else on the planet that possesses your combination of characteristics, experiences, and qualities that make you special. And of course, this is equally true for our kids.

Hence the reason there is no manual telling you how to specifically raise your child and how to respond to their unique needs and wants. There is no one size fits all model to be implemented when we are talking about how our kids react to the world around them.

In a world of differences, this chapter will be focussing on our kids that need a little more support as they see the world differently, have a disability or trauma that impacts their life experiences and opportunities.

But no matter if your child is neurotypical or not, having emotional connections, the need to feel safe, seen, soothed and secure is fundamental to them as well.

It also goes without saying that in the journey of parenthood, one of the most profound and rewarding experiences is watching your child grow, develop, and become their unique selves. Each of our kids are a complex blend of personality traits, talents, and quirks that make them one-of-a-kind.

Some of our kids may have neurological differences that set them apart from what society deems as 'neurotypical'. In this chapter, we'll focus on accepting and embracing our children for who they are and provide some thoughts on how we might do that, regardless of whether they are neurotypical, neurodiverse or impacted by adverse life experiences.

## *The spectrum of neurodiversity*

Neurodiversity is a concept that recognises and celebrates the natural variation in human brain development and functioning. It encompasses a wide range of neurological differences including autism, ADHD, dyslexia, and many others. The neurodiversity movement encourages us to view these conditions not as deficits, but as different ways of experiencing the world.

As parents, in fact anyone who cares for kids, it's essential to understand that neurodiversity exists on a spectrum. Some kids may exhibit characteristics commonly associated with neurodiverse conditions, while others may fall within the neurotypical range. It is is equally crucial to recognise that a child's neurodiversity is just one aspect of their identity and doesn't define their entire being.

Let's take a look at some of the ways we can show our kids we value who they are and that we see them wholistically, not just their differences.

## *Unconditional Love and Acceptance*

Accepting a child for who they are, neurotypical or neurodiverse, begins with unconditional love. Love is the foundation upon which a child's self-esteem and self-worth are built. When you love a child unconditionally, you convey the message that you accept them for who they are, no matter what.

Unconditional love means embracing a child's strengths and weaknesses, quirks and idiosyncrasies, and celebrating their achievements and milestones, no matter how small. It means letting go of preconceived notions of what a 'typical' child should be like and instead cherishing the unique individual the child is becoming.

## *Embracing Differences*

Every child has their own set of strengths and challenges, and this is especially true for neurodiverse children. Instead of trying to fit a child into a mould or comparing them to others, we can simply embrace their differences. Celebrate their unique abilities and talents and support them in overcoming any obstacles they may face.

For neurodiverse children, their differences can be a source of incredible strength. Many individuals with neurodiverse traits have exceptional talents and abilities in areas like mathematics, music, art, and problem-solving. By nurturing and encouraging these strengths, adults can help a child thrive and build self-confidence.

## *Empathy and Understanding*

Empathy and understanding are essential tools in a parent's toolkit when it comes to accepting neurodiversity. Taking the time to learn about how a child sees the world and how it affects them, can be achieved by being open to understanding a child's unique needs by giving them a safe space to be themselves. By empathising with their struggles, frustrations, and challenges parents and carers are letting them know they will show up for them, no matter what.

## *Fostering Self-Acceptance*

Ultimately, one of the most valuable gifts parents and carers can give a child is the ability to accept themselves for who they are. Teaching them that their worth is not determined by their neurodiversity, or any other external factors, helps them develop a strong sense of self, self-esteem and belonging.

Also, by encouraging a child to embrace their strengths and interests, pursue their passions, and set their own goals, lets them know others believe in their abilities and potential. Which in turn manifests into their own self-belief.

### *Cultivating a Supportive Environment*

Acceptance and support should not be confined to the home. It's important to cultivate a supportive environment for our neurodiverse kids in the broader community. This can include their school, extracurricular activities, and social circles.

**School:** working closely with a child's teachers and school staff to create an Individualised Education Plan (IEP) or accommodations that cater to their specific needs is highly beneficial, aswell as ensuring that the school environment is inclusive which assist in promoting understanding among students.

**Extracurricular Activities:** whether it's joining a sports team, participating in drama, or engaging in a hobby, these activities can boost their self-esteem and help neurodiverse kids connect with like-minded peers.

**Social Circles:** building meaningful friendships is fundamental to all human beings to support connection and a sense of belonging. Neurodiverse kids need a little extra support with this, so providing plenty of opportunities to socialise, helps them to understand and practice social cues and navigate social situations.

## *The Power of Language*

The way we talk about neurodiversity can have a significant impact on how kids perceive themselves and how others view them. Being mindful of the language and avoiding stigmatizing or derogatory terms and using person-first language can emphasise a child's individuality rather than their neurodiversity.

Example of some Inclusive Language:

| Language and practice to avoid | Good inclusive language practice |
| --- | --- |
| Special needs | Individual needs |
| Learning impaired | Person with a learning disability |
| Aspie or Asperger's (no longer a diagnosis, so only if someone self identifies), high or low functioning | Person with autism or autistic or neurodivergent (dependent on individual) |
| Challenging, defiant, manipulative, controlling | Dysregulated, experiencing a stress response, having a hard time |

It is equally important to educate those around a neurodiverse child about the importance of respectful and inclusive language. Encouraging family members, friends, and teachers to model inclusive language promotes acceptance and understanding.

## Nurturing Resilience

Resilience is a vital trait for all children, but it can be especially valuable for neurodiverse children who may face additional challenges. Teaching kids problem-solving skills and coping strategies to navigate difficult situations and encouraging them to persevere in the face of adversity is building resilience skills.

It's also essential to create a safe space for a child to express their emotions. This is where you might put into practice all that we have been learning about, that is, showing up for our kids. By letting a child know you see them so that they feel felt it reassures them it's okay to feel frustrated, sad, or overwhelmed at times, and that a caring and reliable adult will be there to help them feel safe and secure.

## Celebrating Achievements

Throughout a child's life journey, taking the time to celebrate their achievements, no matter how small they may seem, is critical as it boosts confidence and motivation.

Creating a system of positive reinforcement, where a child receives praise and rewards for their efforts and accomplishments regularly, demonstrates that they are valued and all milestones, big or small are a victory worth celebrating.

Accepting kids for who they are, whether neurotypical or neurodiverse, is a journey of love, understanding, and growth. When we (parents, carers and wider community) embrace neurodiversity and celebrate a child's unique qualities, we empower them to thrive, build resilience, and make their mark on the world in their own extraordinary way.

## *Seeking Professional Guidance*

Parenting a neurodiverse child or child with additional individual needs can be both rewarding and challenging. There may be moments when parents or carers are uncertain about the best way to support a child's unique needs. During these times, seeking guidance from professionals, such as paediatricians, psychologists, or special education experts, can be invaluable.

Experts can provide insights, strategies, and resources tailored to a child's specific situation and they can also connect parents with support networks and organisations dedicated to neurodiversity advocacy.

## *Support For Kids Who Have Experienced Trauma*

I'd like to switch gears a little and shift our focus towards kids that also need additional support due to circumstance and environment. Unfortunately, a large proportion of kids experience trauma or neglect from a very young age.

A study called the Australian Child Maltreatment Study (ACMS) was conducted recently by a consortium of researchers from Australia, the USA and UK, with the results published in the medical Journal of Australia in April 2023.

*One-of-a-Kind: Recognising the Beauty of Our Uniqueness*

*"The Australian Child Maltreatment Study (ACMS) surveyed 8500 randomly selected Australians aged 16-65 years and over, finding high prevalence of childhood maltreatment experienced by people of every age group.*

*It found that, in childhood aged up to 18:*

*32.0% had experienced physical abuse;*

*28.5% had experienced sexual abuse;*

*30.9% had experienced emotional abuse;*

*8.9% had experienced neglect; and*

*39.6% of respondents had been exposed to domestic violence between parents."* [26]

I am guessing after taking in those statistics, you may be like me and find them to be both startling and shocking! It is also incredibly sobering for what that means for us as a society. My personal opinion is we've got a lot of work to do.

But in this book, we have influence over only what we can do to protect our kids from trauma and traumatic experiences as best we can. We've already called out that parenting is hard and life in general can be hard, so when talking about trauma here, I am referencing the experiences kids have when they are exposed to extensive and prolonged amounts of stress. Not the everyday speed humps and hurdles that we experience that usually last for a short time.

For those of you that are parenting or caring for little people who have experienced trauma, there are a number of things you can do to support them, but fundamentally all that we have talked about applies. Kids who have experienced trauma crave and need to be seen, safe, soothed, and secure.

Trauma can have profound effects on a child's emotional and psychological development, so providing a safe and nurturing environment is crucial. Here are some things that may be helpful to support a child who has experienced trauma:

**Ensure safety and stability:** minimising exposure to ongoing sources of trauma or stress by providing a safe, predictable and stable environment.

**Seeking professional help:** consulting with a mental health professional or therapist experienced in trauma treatment to assess a child's needs is highly recommended. Recommendations may include therapy, counselling, or other interventions.

**Listen and validate:** creating an open and nonjudgmental space for a child to express their feelings and thoughts enables an environment where their feelings and experiences are validated and lets them know it's okay to feel the way they do.

**Maintain a routine:** establishing and maintaining a consistent daily routine with predictability can help provide a sense of safety and control.

**Provide reassurance and comfort:** offering comfort and physical affection when a child is upset or distressed can reassure them they are loved and cared for.

**Educate yourself:** educating yourself about the effects of trauma on children and the specific type of trauma the child has experienced will give you a deeper understanding and potentially help you provide better support.

**Avoid triggers:** being aware of potential triggers for the child's trauma reactions and try to minimise exposure to these triggers.

**Encourage healthy coping strategies:** teaching a child a healthy way to cope with their emotions, such as deep breathing, mindfulness exercises, or creative outlets like art or journaling are supportive and beneficial.

**Build a supportive network:** engaging with family, friends, and community resources to create a support network for the child and yourself as the caregiver will mean you are not alone in the journey.

**Be patient and understanding:** understanding that healing from trauma takes time and patience. Avoiding phrases like 'get over it' or 'just move on' and replacing them with words that demonstrate acceptance and validation can support healing and positive progress.

**Monitor for changes:** keep an eye on a child's behaviour, mood, and interactions. What this means is being alert to any signs of worsening distress or the need for additional professional help, that way support can be provided in a timely way.

**Self-care for caregivers:** taking care of well-being for parents and carers is critical, as we just talked about in the previous chapter. Caring for a child who has experienced trauma can be emotionally challenging, so prioritise self-care and seek support for yourself if and when you may need it.

## *Final Thoughts*

Remember that every child is unique, and what works for one may not work for another. Tailoring an approach to a child's individual needs, and consulting with professionals for guidance when it is both appropriate and necessary. Consistent support and understanding can play a significant role in helping a child heal and thrive after experiencing trauma.

Parenting children who are neurodiverse or have additional individual support needs can be a journey filled with sunshine and storms, but remember in those times of challenge, reach out, as there are many amazing organisations and professionals available to support and help navigate the special and unique needs of all kids, not just those that are neurodiverse or who have experienced trauma.

Special note, to those amazing adults that are reading this book who take care of a child or young person who is not in a home with their birth parents, I salute you. You are giving that little person a gift, the gift of a safe, stable, and loving home environment, where they can heal from their past experiences and thrive as they look towards the future. You are AMAZING and THANK YOU!

# Chapter 9

# The Inner Compass: Mastering The 8th Sense - Interoception

*"Our bodies communicate to us clearly and specifically, if we are willing to listen to them."* Shakti Gawain

In this chapter, I want to introduce you to another tool we can pop in our toolkit to help our kids feel connected, safe, seen, and secure. The connection we will be touching on here is about our kids connection to not only others, but to themselves as well. If our kids can develop a connection to their bodies and understand the signals coming from within, they will be more likely to self-regulate and manage their emotions.

As we move throughout our daily activities, our bodies are continually gathering information to inform our actions and responses. For example, think about the smell of bacon cooking in the pan, the flavour of the first sip of that lifesaving coffee, the warmth of a fire on a cold morning or the whining of a hungry child, it's all information that provides us with sensory input. All of this happens automatically for us. For example, we do not consciously have to think about seeing things, it happens as soon as we open our eyes. All of this information gathering occurs millions of times a day, because as humans we are sensory creatures, and we can be grateful to our bodies for the input via our senses.

Back in my classroom teacher days, teaching my students about the five senses was one of my favourite activities to do and when I reflect on why, it was because the kids were fully engaged in the lesson. They loved feeling a range of different fabrics and surfaces, listening to different pieces of music through headphones, tasting different fruits or the occasional M&M, smelling various flowers or looking for different patterns or shapes in their environment. All these activities involved them being aware of their bodies, the sensory information they were receiving, and how it was making them feel.

Of course, we then talked about the five senses, giving them the names of touch, taste, hearing, smell, and sight. These five basic senses are the ones we are most familiar with and are the ones that roll off our tongues when we're asked to identify our senses. Recently, there has been quite a bit of research undertaken in this area of science, and there are a few new kids on the block, in the senses arena. We actually have eight senses. The five just mentioned and then the less familiar three: vestibular (balance), proprioceptive (movement) and interoceptive (internal).

It is the last sense - interoception, we are going to explore in this chapter, as it plays a critical role in how we recognise and manage our emotions. As parents, if we have a little understanding about interoception, it helps us support our kids to feel a greater sense of connection to themselves and others. By paying attention to how our kids bodies are reacting to the world around them, it can help us to know what they might need from us.

By tuning into our kids and trying to understand how they experience the world and how that informs their basic feelings, behaviours, thoughts and emotions, we can work to support their emotional landscape and build secure attachment.

To give a bit of context, I'll share a little of the science and then we'll move into what it looks like.

The concept of interoception has been around for centuries, but it wasn't until the late 19th century and early 20th century that the research became more mainstream.

Leading Australian researcher Dr Emma Goodall (2016) has collaboratively conducted research on interoception and its effects on wellbeing and says:

> *"Other researchers as well as a range of health and education professionals around the world are now confirming that interoception is a pre-requisite for connection to self and others, as well as the ability to self-manage and self-regulate."* [27]

Scientists and researchers have discovered interoceptive signals come from inside our bodies, mainly from the organs like the heart, lungs, stomach, and intestines. These signals travel to the brain through a network of nerves, including the poly vagus nerve and a part of the brain called the insular cortex that's deep in the brain, and it's crucial for dealing with interoceptive signals.

The insular cortex in the brain receives signals about all sorts of bodily feelings, helping us keep tabs on what's going on inside us. It can be as basic as knowing your tummy's rumbling when you're hungry, or as tricky as picking up on changes in your heart rate and breathing when you're stressed or excited. This brain area then processes all this information, helping us make sense of how our bodies feel and use that to guide how we act and react emotionally.

In essence interoception has a big impact on our basic feelings and moods, which is why it is so beneficial for parents to know a little about it. And it can be particularly helpful for parents with a neurodiverse child who might encounter challenges in forming connections with themselves and others.

Super important sense, super important to know about! However from my experience with my own kids and teaching thousands of other children, not once have I explicitly taught kids to listen to the signals their bodies are sending them. Chances are you won't remember being explicitly taught those skills either. It's not a judgment, it's just there was little known about interoception, so it was not very common in mainstream language back in the day. If am brutally honest, a lot of people grew up in families where talking about feelings and emotions was not particularly common or encouraged. People still felt the sensations , but they either ignored, pushed down, or dismissed them as just another body sensation and just got on with it.

Kids with poor interceptive awareness may be oblivious to the array of bodily signals they receive, leading to missed cues and chances to manage their reactions. They may not recognise sensations like hunger, thirst, discomfort, or even pain and can misinterpret certain signals, for example, interpreting 'butterflies in the tummy' as a sign of danger rather than the urge to use the toilet.

So as parents, what we might see on the outside, is a direct result of what's happening on the inside of your little person. We might see externalising behaviours such as fussiness, frustration, and general irritability, which could actually be hunger, but your child is not making that connection. I'm sure we've all seen and or experienced being 'hangry', I know I have and if I don't eat when I'm at my most hungry, things can escalate quickly!

It could also look like restlessness and squirming movements, that distract from what they are doing, that could indicate the potential need to wee, but the child dismisses or doesn't acknowledge those sensations.

It's these signals, that we as parents can tune into and recognise in our kids, so that we can support them to connect with their bodies and their internal sensations, to develop their interoceptive sense.

Mona Delahooke PhD says:

> *"... helping children (and adults) observe and make sense of their bodily sensations is one of the best ways to support self-regulation. Eventually, we can help children label those sensations with emotional or other descriptive words."* [28]

If we can help our kids to develop their interoceptive sense, then we can support them to have more awareness of how they are feeling and how they might respond when things are becoming challenging or overwhelming.

But before we continue, I want to call out that emotions are not a uniform experience. It needs to be acknowledged that our inner experiences are highly individualised and equally valid. For example, what I feel inside my body is distinct from what you feel inside yours. As we talk about what we can do as parents to help our kids develop their interoception sense, be aware that it is a very individual journey. There is no one size fits all.

Interoception is the process we as humans move through multiple times a day and is applicable to children and adults alike. For some it is automatic and for others it takes time to develop and strengthen the sense, which is totally ok. The bottom line is that all emotions and sensations need to be acknowledged and honoured, as it helps us to regulate and connect with those around us.

The image over the page provides an overview of the stages we move through via our interoceptive sense.

Let's take a closer look at the five stages of interoception and what each means.

*The Inner Compass: Mastering The 8th Sense - Interoception*

# 5 STAGES OF INTEROCEPTION

**1. Noticing:**
Noticing involves being mindful of these sensations without judgment or evaluation. It's about simply observing what is happening within your body.

**2. Naming:**
Naming the sensations helps you develop a more precise and articulated understanding of what's happening in your body.

**3. Linking feelings:**
Linking feelings helps you recognise the mind-body connection and understand how your body responds to various emotional triggers.

**4. Understanding the impact:**
Understanding the impact involves gaining insight into how your body's signals and sensations influence your behaviour, mood, and overall well-being.

**5. Managing:**
Learning to manage and regulate your bodily sensations and emotional responses.

## 1. Noticing:

During the noticing stage, you pay attention to the various bodily sensations and signals you experience throughout the day. These sensations can include things like heart rate, muscle tension, breathing patterns, temperature changes, and visceral feelings like hunger or fatigue.

Noticing involves being mindful of these sensations without judgment or evaluation. It's about simply observing what is happening within your body.

## 2. Naming:

After noticing these bodily sensations, the next step is to give them names or labels. This involves identifying and categorising the specific sensations you're feeling. For example, you might notice that your heart rate has increased, or you might recognise a tightness in your chest.

Naming the sensations helps develops a more precise and articulated understanding of what's happening in your body.

## 3. Linking Feelings:

In this stage, you connect these bodily sensations with your emotional and cognitive experiences. You become aware of how your physical sensations are linked to your feelings and thoughts. For example, you may notice that a racing heart is often associated with feelings of anxiety or excitement.

Linking feelings helps you recognise the mind-body connection and understand how your body responds to various emotional triggers.

## 4. Understanding the Impact:

Understanding the impact involves gaining insight into how your body's signals and sensations influence your behaviour, mood, and overall well-being. You recognise how your body's responses can either support or hinder your daily life.

For instance, you might realise that a racing heart during stressful situations negatively impacts your ability to focus or make decisions.

## 5. Managing:

The final stage of interoceptive awareness involves learning to manage and regulate your bodily sensations and emotional responses. This can include implementing strategies like deep breathing exercises, progressive muscle relaxation, meditation, or other mindfulness techniques.

By managing our interoceptive awareness, we can develop greater emotional regulation, reduce stress, and make healthier choices in response to body signals.

Whilst it sounds tricky and complicated, it's not really, it just requires some self-awareness, and our interception sense develops and becomes automatic as we grow and learn to manage ourselves.

So, what are some of the signals we need to be on the lookout for that may be affecting our child's ability to self-regulate their behaviour and emotions? This not an exhaustive list, but what we may see includes:

- frowning
- raised eyebrows
- clenched jaws
- sweaty red face
- slumped shoulders
- crossed arms
- fidgeting
- avoiding eye contact
- raised voice
- soft voice or almost inaudible tone
- blushing (reddening of the cheeks)
- sweating
- pupil dilation
- rapid or shallow breathing
- tremors or shaking in the hands or body
- teeth chattering

I'm sure we can all relate to these 'behaviours' as adults and have potentially seen them in our kids.

The creators of the Circle of Security, a relationship-based parenting program, with nurturing secure attachment at the very centre of the approach, frequently talk about 'what's hidden in plain sight'. And what they mean by hidden in plain sight is our kids are giving us clues they need our support; they need us to show up for them in that moment and some of those clues could be many of those mentioned above. The Circle of Security approach, is about being aware and open to not quickly labelling these clues as behaviour but viewing them as a way our kids are asking for our help.

Often there are quick ways we can support, such as offering warm clothing if they are cold, or teaching breathing techniques to restore calm. But one of the easiest things we can do to help our child develop their interoceptive sense is encourage them to use their words to notice and name the sensations and emotions. We can help them do this by making observations and asking questions. For example:

- I can see your face is red and you're frowning. I wonder where you feel that in your body?
- I notice you are fidgety and restless. Are you feeling uncomfortable?
- Do you feel something in your body?
- Oh, I notice that you're shaking. I wonder what's going on.

Another powerful way to support our kids to develop this sense is for us to model or talk out loud about how we are feeling - noticing, naming it and linking the feeling to it. For example:

- My mouth is very dry, I must need some water.
- My stomach is growling, and I have a little pain, I might need to eat some food.
- My body feels tired, and I am yawning, I think I need a nap.

The power of this, especially for our very little kids or our kids who may be nonverbal, is that we know they are taking in what's going on around them, which includes language and behaviour. Never underestimate a child's ability to take on language. I don't know how many times I've seen a mum or dad reel with horror when their little one drops a contextually perfect F bomb out in public. I'm sure you can all relate. And I have to admit, when I am witness to that, on the inside I giggle a little, and say YES! That little one has a firm grasp on language and knows how to use it. (Once a teacher always a teacher, I guess)

So along with the everyday moments that are presented multiple times a day, there are also some fun ways and more deliberate ways to help our kids develop their 8th sense.

Here's 10 interoception activities to try which are suitable for little ones that are simple, engaging, and age-appropriate to help them develop a basic understanding of their internal sensations.

**1. Breathing Buddies:** have your child lie down with a stuffed animal or a small toy on their belly. Ask them to watch how it rises and falls with each breath. This helps them connect breathing with body movements.

**2. Feelings Faces:** create a chart or cards with different facial expressions representing various emotions. Ask your child to point to or mimic the face that matches how they're feeling. Talk about the physical sensations that accompany those emotions.

**3. Sensory Play:** engage in sensory activities like playing with sand, water, or play dough. Encourage them to describe how it feels and how their hands and body respond to the sensory experience.

**4. Musical Freeze Dance:** play music and encourage your child to dance. When the music stops, ask them to freeze and notice how their heart is beating and how their breath feels in their body.

**5. Emotion Mirroring:** make funny faces in a mirror together and ask the child to mirror your expressions. Discuss how different emotions make their faces and bodies feel.

**6. Feeling Thermometer:** create a 'feeling thermometer' with various emotion faces from happy to sad. Ask the child to point to the face that matches how they're feeling and talk about any physical sensations they notice.

**7. Breathing with Shapes:** use simple shapes like circles or squares. As they trace the shape with their finger, encourage them to take a deep breath in for one side and exhale for the other, helping them connect breath with movement.

**8. Hugging Exercise:** have the child give themselves a gentle hug and ask how it feels. This activity can help them notice the sensations of touch and pressure on their bodies.

**9. Balloon Breath:** pretend their belly is a balloon. Inhale and imagine inflating the balloon, then exhale slowly, letting the air out. This helps them connect breath and body expansion.

**10. Emotion Stories:** read picture books or tell stories that feature characters experiencing different emotions. Pause to discuss how the characters might be feeling in their bodies.

Keep in mind that young children have limited attention spans, so keep these activities short and playful. These fun activities will help them begin to recognise and understand their internal sensations and emotions, leading to increased ability to self-regulate and feeling connected to themselves and others.

So, there you have it. We are blessed with not just five senses but eight. There continues to be more and more information out there about interception and the benefits of helping our kids to develop it. I've given you an overview here but a simple search on the internet will yield lots of information.

It's also important to remember as we've talked about in previous chapters, that dysregulation is a normal part of childhood development, and occasional displays of these behaviours are common. However, if your child consistently shows dysregulation that significantly interferes with their daily functioning or well-being, it may be helpful to seek support from a professional who specialises in child development and emotional regulation. Early intervention and strategies to support emotional regulation can be highly beneficial for children struggling with these challenges.

See you over the page.

# Chapter 10

# Creating Moments of Magic: Embracing The Power of Play

*"Play is the highest form of research"* – Albert Einstein

Throughout my career as a teacher and school leader, I have participated in thousands of hours of professional learning, certifications, and study to extend my knowledge and cater to the needs of the kids in my class.

I've viewed hundreds of videos and clips geared towards child development and learning, and there are a handful of videos that have stuck in my mind and have had a huge impact on me and have transformed my teaching and parenting style.

One of those videos I have already shared with you back in Chapter 4, called the Still Face Experiment and, as you may recall, it was a little distressing. But the video I want to share with you now and encourage you to watch, is beautiful and contains a very powerful message delivered by Molly Wright, a seven-year-old child, in her Ted talk called, "How every child can thrive by five". Yes you read that correctly. Molly was just seven years old when she delivered her TED talk and she is still one of the youngest speakers ever.

I'll let Molly tell you in her words what she believes kids need from their parents in order to thrive.

> "Our healthy development depends on these top five things: one, connecting; two, talking; three, playing; four, a healthy home, five, community. All of this helps our brains and us reach our full potential." [29] (2021)

Pretty insightful stuff for a seven-year-old, wouldn't you agree? And I'm guessing it's also the reason the video stayed with me. This was not the voice of an adult, but the voice of a child who is telling us as adults, this is what she needs to grow and develop into a healthy adult.

When I look at Molly's list, we have touched on most of her top five things, but there is one that we haven't talked about yet and it is in my top five also. In this chapter, I'd like to explore with you the importance of play and how critical it is to our kids' development and wellbeing.

As with all things, we have our own understanding and interpretation of concepts, so when I say 'play', I'm guessing you will more than likely have a visual in your head of what play looks like to you. It could be an image of kids playing a game of football, jumping on a trampoline or a child playing a video game, all totally legit examples of play.

But to stretch things a little, I'd like to plant the seed that play is all of those things, but it is also a powerful tool to support a child's overall development, including their cognitive, social and emotional wellbeing.

Researcher Yogman et al(2018).; in his clinical report to paediatricians says:

> *"Research demonstrates that developmentally appropriate play with parents and peers is a singular opportunity to promote the social and emotional, cognitive, language and self-regulation skills that build executive functioning and a pro social brain."* [30]

What that means is, kids playing with their parents or mates, helps them to use their pro social brains to restore calm, be cooperative, solve problems, and see other people's point of view. This also helps them to develop their executive functioning skills, such as the ability to display self-control, follow simple instructions and maintain focus. All skills that we want for our kids now and for later in life.

Pretty amazing right! But the best thing of all about this is, play is available to all of us and does not have to cost a cent to engage with it. In today's world, play can be VERY expensive, think video consoles and handheld devices. Whilst those items have a place and most definitely form part of our kids' world of play, there are so many other things available at our fingertips that don't cost a bomb, that support and enable play.

As a realist, I am making an assumption now that you are probably thinking at this point,

"Oh man, play, how and I am going to find time to do that with my kid, along with the million other things I need to get done?".

If this is you, I feel you. This was me too. The struggle is real.

Even now, when I am bogged down with work and think, I'll just get this done and play with Hudson later, I stop and remind myself of another of my favourite quotes, this time from author Zig Zigler, when he says;

*"To a child love is spelled T.I.M.E."* [31]

Time, it's the one thing all parents struggle with, but if taken, can reap huge rewards for your child and your relationship with them. It nurtures and nourishes their feeling of safety and builds their sense of belonging and secure attachment. But don't stress, it doesn't need to be hours of play, it can just be a few minutes a day and there is no need for fancy devices or toys. The key ingredient here is YOU.

The other great thing is just five minutes a day of uninterrupted play with your child has a multitude of health benefits for the both of you. Your child's emotional landscape will flourish, and you will have the opportunity to indulge your inner child, which sadly, for most of us, doesn't get to see the light of day very often.

Again, don't stress, even though you are key, it doesn't mean that you have to be the one instigating and entertaining. In fact, following our child's lead in play can be incredibly insightful. Through child-led play, they give us a window into what they may be worrying about, what's on their minds and what they may need extra help with, such as interoceptive development.

*Creating Moments of Magic: Embracing The Power of Play*

These things can be observed, but we can also pick up on these clues through their language and the words they are using in play.

Mona Delhooke PhD(2022) shares her thoughts on the power of play, she says:

> "…play offers a powerful way to connect with your child with safety and joy - and a chance to have fun together while getting a window into the child's interest and concerns. Don't feel like you have to fix anything about the child during play…. This is part of the magic of play: Children can experiment with concepts, ideas, and emotions outside of 'real' life, but in a simulation of their own making. The power of that simulation can't be underestimated." [32]

This is particularly helpful to know and be aware of because it is par for the course that during play, a range of negative and positive emotions will come through. As a parent, it is nothing to be afraid of if negative emotions arise. On the contrary, it's actually a great sign, as it shows that your child is working through the emotions, which may be difficult to work on in real life.

If your child includes negative emotions, as difficult and challenging as it may be at times, try to observe more than teach during these moments. But of course, if you or your child are unsafe, especially if there is physical hitting or lashing out, setting those respectful boundaries is necessary and appropriate.

Also remember, play does not always need to be structured and scheduled. In fact, there is concern amongst professionals that kids' lives nowadays are way too scheduled. Some kids and families are involved in many 'extra' activities outside preschool and school, with parents wanting to provide their kids with enriching experiences. However, there is a growing trend towards decreasing the number of planned activities, as excessive structured time might hinder kids' opportunities to cultivate crucial skills, such as learning to handle things independently.

To learn more about play and the benefits of play, I recommend checking out the National Institute of Play (NIP). NIP is a corporation established by Dr Stuart Brown, a psychiatrist, who has devoted his life to learning about and understanding play.

The NIP website houses a plethora of information and research and calls out explicitly that play has a critical role in fostering healthy and fulfilling lives, regardless of age. It has become evident that play holds a real significance for mental well-being, which is equivalent to that of the importance of food for physical health.

*Creating Moments of Magic: Embracing The Power of Play*

There are eight areas of evidence that the research says are critical to human development, some of them will be familiar to you, as we have covered them in previous chapters, but indulge me for a moment as I highlight them again and briefly explain what each of them mean:

1. **Babies Need Attunement Play to Learn and Grow**
   In the initial stages of a baby's life, parents instinctively initiate a form of interaction known as 'attunement'. During these shared moments, for example, gazing into each other's eyes, parents and babies establish a profound connection. This early attunement in infancy serves as a pivotal factor in fostering emotional self-regulation during childhood and sets the groundwork for continued learning and growth from the toddler years all the way through adolescence.

2. **Play Builds More Complex Brains**
   We talked a lot about this in chapter 2 and as you'll recall, over 70% of the neural pathway wiring is completed by the time a child is three years old and the message here is that play is critically important to creating and establishing that wiring.

3. **Babies Learn by Moving**
   Moving around and playing is a big part of how we grow and shape our brains. Babies start this kind of play when they wave their arms and kick their legs. As they grow, they figure out how to rock, roll over, and crawl on their hands and knees. They also like sticking things in their mouths and playing with their food. This kind of play helps them to learn about the world.

**4. Play = Learning**
Babies and toddlers start building their play skills in response to what's happening around them. Even newborns, in their first few months, develop brain connections as they figure out how to move and interact with their fingers, arms, and legs. Eventually, this exploration leads them to move around and explore their surroundings to learn from them.

**5. Play Develops Emotional Intelligence (EQ)**
We discussed EQ extensively in chapter six. By allowing kids plenty of unstructured free playtime and nurturing their natural inclination to play with others they learn to navigate the various challenges and emotions that come up in social interactions, including how to manage their own emotions.

**6. Kids Need Rough-and-Tumble Play**
Rough-and-tumble play involves physical contests aimed at gaining an advantage but should not be confused with actual fighting. Sometimes, adults may try to discourage kids from engaging in rough-and-tumble play out of concern for potential injuries. However, as long as everyone is having fun, and there's no violence or threats involved, rough-and-tumble play offers several benefits for kids.

**7. Play Deprivation Can Have Tragic Consequences**
The research into play deprivation is sobering, Dr Stuart Brown states:

*"...sustained, moderate to severe play deprivation particularly during the first 10 years of life, is linked to major emotional dysregulation, i.e., increased prevalence of depression, a tendency to become inflexible in thought, diminished impulse control, less self-regulation, poor management of aggression, and fragility and shallowness of enduring interpersonal relationships."* (Brown S.L. 2014) Heavy and confronting information! Underlying message here - let your kids play and play often.

8. **Play Improves Lives:**
   Play has the power to enhance our mental well-being, boost our ability to connect with others, and ignite our motivation and optimism for the future. While play may not work magic to solve every issue, it can, and undoubtedly will, provide you and your kids with a brighter perspective and help reduce stress levels when navigating challenging life circumstances.

The table over the page and content is sourced directly from the NIP website and I acknowledge the work of Dr Stuart Brown (2014).

| When Life is | Play-Filled | Play-Deprived |
|---|---|---|
| Trust | Life is experienced as a playground filled with chances to learn | Life is experienced as a proving ground — and often a battleground |
| Flexibility | Change brings exploration and new possibilities | Change creates fear and resistance |
| Optimism | Well-being and pleasure are expected | Discomfort and disappointment are expected |
| Problem-Solving | Problems are acknowledged and often foster skill development | Problems are hidden, denied, or avoided |
| Emotional Regulation | Stress is handled with resilience; the response is most often stability | Stress responses are often anger, rage, or withdrawal caused by low self-efficacy |
| Perseverance | Motivation is sustained from internal drive, mastery is sought | Motivation dissipates; equivocation, procrastination, and apathy arise |
| Empathy | Others' feelings are recognised; support is often offered | Others' feelings are not recognised; discord occurs |
| Openness | Life is vital; a strong sense of belonging fosters social cooperation | Life is dull; people become socially withdrawn, often with mild depression |

| Belonging | Behaviours are altruistic, leading to teamwork, community creation, and participation | Behaviours are callous, uncooperative, bullying, and self-centred |

I've given you lots of information to take on here, but the underlying key message throughout is that play is critical to our kids' development. Just as we have a 9-5 job, our kids' day job is to learn about their world, and the most natural and beneficial way for them to do that is through play. As you can see from the table above, there are so many benefits, including establishing trust, a sense of belonging and the ability to self-regulate.

Without regular and frequent opportunities for play, our kids experience the world from an entirely different perspective, seeing life as a constant challenge, being uncooperative and responding to situations in an escalated way.

If thinking about play in this way, is new to you, it can seem a little overwhelming, and you may be thinking, *ok where do I start?* So, to get you underway, here's a list of simple and easy games you can play with your child, that only takes a few minutes and I can guarantee your child will love them!

## 20 Fun and Easy Games to Play

1. **Hide and Seek:** the classic game where one person hides while the other counts, then tries to find them.
2. **Simon Says:** give simple commands like, "Simon says touch your toes," or "Simon says clap your hands." If you don't say "Simon says," before the command, they shouldn't do it.
3. **Nature Scavenger Hunt:** go for a walk in a park or your backyard and look for specific natural items like leaves, rocks, or flowers.
4. **Storytelling:** encourage your child to make up their own stories, or you can take turns creating a story together.
5. **Dress-Up:** let them explore your closet and dress up in different clothes and costumes.
6. **Pretend Play:** encourage imaginative play by pretending to be animals, pirates, or other characters.
7. **Building with Blocks:** use building blocks or even empty cardboard boxes to build towers, houses, or anything else they can imagine.
8. **Art and Craft Time:** get creative with paper, crayons, markers, and other art supplies. You can create drawings, paintings, or simple crafts like paper plate masks.
9. **Cook Together:** involve your child in simple cooking or baking tasks, like making cookies or sandwiches.
10. **Music and Dance:** put on some music and dance together. You can also make simple musical instruments, like shakers from rice-filled containers.
11. **Sensory Play:** fill a bin with rice, beans, or sand and provide scoops and containers for them to explore and play with.

12. **Outdoor Play:** head to the local playground or simply play in your backyard. Activities like swinging, sliding, and playing catch are always fun.
13. **Yoga for Kids:** look for kid-friendly yoga routines on YouTube and do some simple yoga poses together.
14. **Freeze Dance:** play music and dance around. When you pause the music, everyone has to freeze in place until the music starts again.
15. **Picnic:** have an indoor or outdoor picnic with their favourite snacks and sandwiches.
16. **Bubbles:** blow bubbles and let them chase and pop them. You can make your own bubble solution with dish soap and water.
17. **Reading Time:** read books together. You can take turns reading or make up stories based on the pictures in the book.
18. **Colouring Pages:** print out free colouring pages from the internet or draw your own pictures for them to colour.
19. **Obstacle Course:** set up a simple obstacle course using cushions, pillows, and other household items for them to climb over, under, and around.
20. **Memory Game:** place a few items on a tray, let them look at it for a minute, then cover it and see how many items they can remember.

Whilst this is a great list to have and refer to, the most important thing to remember here is that it is not the 'thing' or the 'game' it's the time you get to spend being present with your child, that's where the magic of play is most powerful.

And just in case I haven't made it clear up until now, play occurs anywhere and everywhere and does not always have to involve you as a parent. Our kids need time to explore independently, play with new and different people and make sense of their world in a way that is safe, but also challenging enough for them to grow. This is known as self-directed play and self-directed play has some fantastic benefits including: boosting confidence, encouraging independence, speaking imagination, teaching problem solving, fuelling curiosity and providing control over the pace of learning.

So, there you have it, the magic and power of play! The benefits of it cannot be underestimated. It is an integral part of childhood, offering kids essential developmental advantages while giving you as a parent the chance to actively connect with your kids.

And on that note, I'll leave you with this quote:

> *"Children need the freedom and time to play. Play is not a luxury. Play is a necessity."* — *Kay Redfield Jamison.* [34]

PS. Don't forget to check out Molly Wright's TED talk (link in references section)

# Chapter 11

# Pandemic Fallout: How to Support Through Challenging Times

*"There is a crack in everything. That's how the light gets in."*
*– Leonard Cohen*

Mental health, I'm guessing it's a term you have all heard before. Mental health can be hard to talk about and can make people feel uncomfortable talking about it. I'd like to give you a heads up that this chapter is going to touch on mental health and the growing needs of our school aged kids and young people, because of what can only be described as a significant global health challenge that began in 2019, aka COVID-19. We are also going to talk about ways to support our kids to manage and thrive post pandemic.

You are probably wondering why I would include a chapter about the global pandemic. After all how does it relate to raising happy and emotionally connected kids? Well, a lot, because if we go back to the very core of the topics we have covered so far, the fundamental things that kids need most is to feel; SAFE, SEEN, SOOTHED and SECURE. It it doesn't take too much time to work out which of those things have been compromised for some of our kids, because of COVID-19 and the management of it.

At the time of writing this book, sadly, many of our school aged kids are feeling far less connected, emotionally safe and secure and this can be attributed directly to that event which was completely out of anyone's control. Hence, the reason I felt it was necessary to address the fallout of COVID-19, as the trauma many adults, young people and children have experienced will have mental health repercussions for years to come.

Now to be super clear, I am not a psychologist, therefore the content of this chapter is not about providing psychological advice and support, but rather looking at how we can support our kids to feel safe and emotionally connected through the everyday things we do at home or school.

*\*\* The caveat here though is; if your child (or you for that matter) is experiencing persistent and ongoing symptoms such as anxiety or feeling down, seeking professional support and help is highly recommended.*

### What's the change for some of our kids?

While the virus took a physical toll, the mental well-being of some of our kids also took a heavy hit. Because suddenly everything looked and sounded different. Overnight, we were asked to keep a safe distance from people, wear masks and use copious amounts of hand sanitiser! All very different ways of being and living, which for us as adults was difficult enough to process, let alone a child who is trying to understand the world around them with a brain that is still developing!

As we know our kids rely on a sense of certainty, safety, and the comfort of their daily routines. So, when those routines were disrupted, such as closing of schools, the inability to see grandparents and friends, and cancelling all events that involved interactions with others outside of the immediate family, it destabilised the emotional health of many.

So, for our kids during the pandemic, a common experience was missing out on the things that help them grow and learn. A significant amount of their development happens when they hang out with different caring adults, spend time with all kinds of friends, and get to try new and exciting stuff. But because of the pandemic, they lost out on all of that. Their lives became limited, with most activities happening at home. While it kept them safe from COVID-19, it took away the fun and interesting parts of that growing up period that they really need.

Working as an educator means seeing firsthand how the pandemic has affected and continues to affect our kids. There are a number of telling observations, being reported across all education settings in Australia, such as, but not limited to:

- Increase in the incidences of school refusal.
- Decrease in the number of young kids coming to school who can self-regulate.
- Increase in the number of young kids who have yet to develop basic social skills.

- Increased number of kids reporting feeling anxious and worried about the future.
- Increased addiction to gaming due to the rise in the amount of time spent gaming during the pandemic, to manage their emotional distress and avoid social isolation.

Whilst the observations are a little confronting, it's very easy to understand the why of each of them. Hence, returning to what was the norm before the pandemic has been and continues to be difficult for some of our kids and equally difficult and worrying for their parents.

So, I guess the million-dollar question is, how do I support my child if they are displaying some or any of the observations mentioned above?

Great question, but before we jump into some possible ways, I want to reiterate, there is no judgment attached to any behaviours. They are purely an outcome of a significant world event that has impacted on an individual level.

Below are some suggestions to support overall mental health and further along are some strategies to support behaviours. All the while acknowledging, every child is different, so it's not a one size fits all, but some things to be aware of and possibly try.

## *Overall strategies to support mental health:*

1. **Firstly, look after your own mental health.** Taking care of yourself can be the best way to reassure your kids

during these times. Our kids, as we know, pick up on our emotions, so make sure you're in a good mental space. Practicing self-care sets a positive example for them.

2. **Encourage your child to open up about their feelings.** Sometimes young children find it hard to express themselves, so initiate conversations with gentle and non-judgmental questions like, "How do you feel about going back to school or to the supermarket?" This lets them know their emotions are okay. Remember, it's common for kids to have anxiety after a big event like a pandemic.
3. **Stick to routines and consistency.** Kids thrive on knowing what to expect. Keep up with morning and bedtime routines and try to pick them up from school at the same time. Research shows that having family meals together is good for mental well-being.
4. **Gradually reintroduce familiar activities.** Take small steps, instead of jumping into big indoor gatherings, consider outdoor playdates. Choose settings that your child feels comfortable in.
5. **Talk to them about safety measures.** Involve your child in conversations about what makes them feel safe. Explaining safety measures helps them trust that you're looking out for them.
6. **Celebrate the positive.** Look for the good things your child is doing. Sometimes, we focus too much on what they aren't doing
7. **Get help if needed**. If your child continues to struggle, reach out to their paediatrician, a school counsellor, or a therapist.

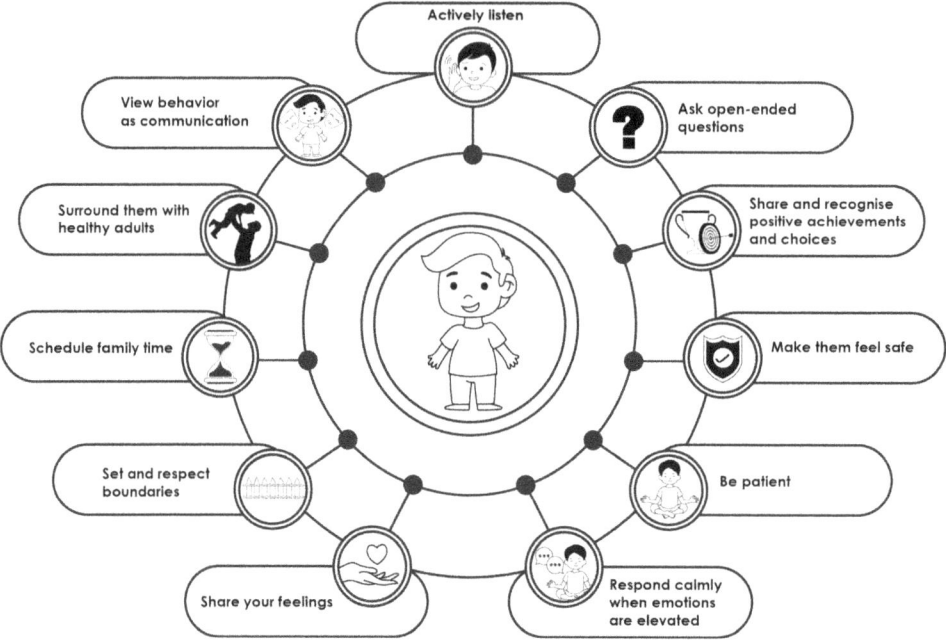

Ways to nuture a child's mental health

## *School Refusal*

If you remember back to your school days, we all had days when we didn't feel like going to school, and it is the same for our kids now, but in current times there's a whole different ball game called 'school refusal'. It's not just about wanting to skip school occasionally; it's when a child or young person has a serious problem with going to school.

What school refusal might look like for a child or young person:

**Duration:** avoiding school for quite a while.
**Distress**: becomes quite upset at the thought of going to school.
**Resistance:** put up a strong resistance to leaving the house and going to school.
**Interference:** school avoidance behaviours start impacting not only their life but also their family routines and activities.

It's not just about missing a day or two of school; it can be about being late all the time because their anxiety makes them late, or they might make a habit of leaving early, hanging out in the sick bay, or texting their parents all day long. That's when you know it's more than just a regular case of, "I don't want to go to school today."

**Ways to support school refusal:**

1. **Find out what's going on for them:** sometimes, it can be tricky to figure out why your child is feeling anxious. The first step is offer to help them figure out what's bothering them exactly. Once you know what's going on, you'll be in a better position to make changes that can help. Think back to the iceberg analogy - what's happening below the surface for them?
2. **Start a conversation with the school:** once you have a bit of an understanding of what may be going on, contact the school and seek their support to develop a supportive plan.
3. **Try starting a morning routine:** having a regular routine for waking up, getting dressed, having breakfast,

and getting ready to leave the house can make everyone feel more secure and less stressed, including you. Try doing some prep work the night before, like checking your child's schedule, packing their bags, and laying out their clothes. In the morning, focus on one step at a time as you follow their schedule, instead of worrying too much about the big goal of 'getting to school'.

4. **Discuss ways to make the school day a little more manageable**: for younger kids, taking a beloved toy from home to school or using a worry box at home can be comforting and help them manage their anxieties. For young people, they might find it helpful to have small sensory items in their pocket to help soothe and focus their mind on.

5. **Encourage fun activities after school:** it's important to have some chill time after school. Encourage things like hanging out with friends and family, listening to favourite music, taking a walk or jog, playing sports, baking, doodling, or just kicking back and watching a movie.

6. **Celebrate the small wins:** keep an eye out for the little victories, like getting up on time or submitting schoolwork, and letting your child know how proud you are of them.

7. **Ease the pressure a little:** there might be days when your child finds it tough to handle leaving home or doing schoolwork. It's important to understand that their mood can have its ups and downs, and you can always give it another shot the following day.

## Ways to support Self-regulation:

We discussed self-regulation at length in chapter five, but see below for some more suggestions to try if your child is struggling to self soothe and regulate whilst at school:

1. **Talk to your child's teacher:** often dysregulation looks like poor behaviour, but as we now know, all behaviour is communication, so it's important to talk to the teacher to understand what they are observing.
2. **Develop a plan together with the school:** you know your child best, so it is important to work with the school to develop a plan to support your child to self-regulate, with the help of the teacher of course (through co-regulation).
3. **Co-regulate at home:** bring the contagious calm to escalating situations at home, model the behaviour we want for our kids as they will mirror it.
4. **Encourage emotion awareness:** help your child identify and label their emotions. Use emotional language to describe what they are feeling. Encourage them to express their feelings by asking questions like, "How are you feeling right now?" or "Can you tell me what's bothering you?"

By supporting self-regulation at home, it will become more evident in the school setting and your child will feel a greater sense of calm and self-awareness.

## *Ways to support social skills:*

Social skills are what we use every day to chat and connect with others. They cover talking and how we express ourselves without words, through our expressions and body language. Someone is considered to have strong social skills if they know how to act in social situations and get both the written and unspoken rules of talking to others. Social skills take time for our little people to develop and can be especially challenging for kids or young people who are neurodiverse or have an intellectual disability.

Here are a few things to consider and try if your child is struggling with social activities and how to be with others:

1. **Play:** spend time playing with your child to help them learn how to share, take turns, find common interests, cooperate, and play nicely with toys.
2. **Talk about emotions**: when it comes to emotions, support your child in understanding and expressing their own feelings, as well as recognising how others feel.
3. **Empathy:** teach empathy by helping your child understand and identify the emotions of others in different situations.
4. **Use social stories**: these are like special stories that help kids grasp tricky social skills. They work by describing specific situations and suggesting the right social responses.
5. **Teach them to ask questions:** asking questions that don't have just a yes or no answer can help to create connection and helps us to understand what others think and feel.

6. **Recognise and appreciate your child's efforts:** show appreciation to your child when they show friendliness and consideration toward others.
7. **Assist with language:** give your kids help with using words to express their desires and emotions, like saying, "I'd like a turn with that," or "Do you want to play with me in the sandpit?"

Social skills are super important for having good interactions with others and building and keeping friendships. But the reality is, not all social interactions go smoothly. So, it's important for our kids to know how to handle tricky situations, like resolving conflicts when they pop up. By teaching and supporting our kids to develop their social skills, they are more likely to develop lasting relationships and feel a deeper sense of connection and belonging.

## *Ways to support an anxious or worried child:*

Anxiety is a common emotion, and it's something we all experience occasionally. In fact, a bit of anxiety can be helpful, as it keeps us alert to potential dangers.

Feeling nervous about an upcoming test or a dance performance, for instance, is a typical part of growing up. Many children experience these anxieties, but if they can still manage to go through with it — take the test or perform at the concert — it falls within the realm of normalcy.

*\*\* However, if a child is so overwhelmed that they're curled up in bed and unable to attend school or engage in typical activities like*

*socialising with friends, interacting with teachers, or performing well academically, that's when it's most concerning and may require professional help.*

But there are some things that parents can do to support and help their child manage some of the anxiety and worry:

1. **Open communication:** create a safe and non-judgmental space for your child to express their feelings and fears. Encourage them to talk about what's bothering them.
2. **Listen actively:** when your child shares their concerns, listen attentively and empathetically. Let them know you understand by saying something like, "I get it, you're feeling anxious, and that's totally okay."
3. **Breathing exercises:** teach your child simple deep-breathing techniques. Breathing slowly and deeply can help calm the nervous system. For example, you can practice balloon breathing where they imagine filling their belly like a balloon when inhaling and deflating it when exhaling.
4. **Mindfulness and meditation:** mindfulness and meditation exercises can help kids become more aware of their thoughts and feelings, reducing anxiety.
5. **Set up a daily schedule:** kids often feel more secure when they know what to expect, and having a regular routine helps with that sense of security.
6. **Limit exposure to stressors:** be mindful of the media content your child is exposed to, and limit exposure to frightening or distressing news or entertainment.
7. **Encourage positive self-talk:** help your child spot and overcome negative thoughts. Encourage them

to replace anxious thoughts with more positive and rational ones.
8. **Physical activity:** encourage your child to engage in physical activities they enjoy.
9. **Create a 'Worry Time':** designate a specific time each day as worry time where your child can express their concerns. Outside of this time, encourage them to set worries aside.
10. **Lead by example:** as we know, children often model their behaviour after adults. Show them how you cope with stress and anxiety in healthy ways to provide a positive example.

As mentioned earlier, if anxiety significantly interferes with your child's daily life, or if you notice persistent signs like severe mood changes or physical symptoms, consider consulting a mental health professional for guidance and support.

## *Ways to Support and Manage Gaming*:

The lockdowns during the pandemic caused significant social isolation and many children, young people and adults turned to screens to ease loneliness, boredom and increase connection. However, the research is now telling us and we are seeing it at schools, there has been a spike in gaming addiction amongst our kids and young people, which is impacting their daily routines. Some things you may see if your child is spending great amounts of time gaming include; reduced sleep, not engaging in other preferred activities, becoming aggressive when game time is minimised, poor personal hygiene and reduced attendance at school. This is not an exhaustive list but things to be mindful of.

Managing gaming, especially for children and teenagers, is important for maintaining a healthy balance between screen time and other activities.

1. **Set Clear Limits and Boundaries:**
    - Establish specific rules for gaming, including the time allowed each day or week.
    - Create a gaming schedule that aligns with schoolwork, chores, and other responsibilities.
    - Encourage breaks during gaming sessions to prevent excessive screen time.

2. **Monitor Game Content:**
    - Familiarise yourself with the content of the games your child is playing.
    - Use age-appropriate rating systems to guide game choices.
    - Discuss and set guidelines for playing games with violent, inappropriate, or addictive content.

3. **Encourage Offline Activities:**
    - Promote a variety of offline activities, such as physical exercise, reading, hobbies, and socialising with friends in person.
    - Offer alternative entertainment options to reduce the temptation of constant gaming.

4. **Lead by Example:**
    - Show your child a balanced approach to screen time by modelling responsible device use.
    - Engage in joint activities that don't involve screens, fostering family connections.

### 5. Use Parental Controls and Technology:
- Utilise parental control features on gaming consoles, computers, and mobile devices to enforce time limits and content restrictions.
- Explore third-party software and apps that provide additional control over screen time and online interactions.

The most important thing to remember is that open communication is key when implementing these strategies. Discuss the reasons behind the rules and boundaries with your child, emphasising the importance of a healthy balance between gaming and other aspects of life, maintaining the relationship with your child is critical.

In summary, as parents, we play a crucial role in supporting our kid's mental health. Making it a priority is highly beneficial because it lays the foundation for lifelong well-being and helps our kids develop the skills and resilience necessary to navigate the challenges of life.

The underlying message here is that our mental health is a priority also, as our kids need us to show up and provide the secure base that they crave. But in saying that, life is challenging and can throw us curve balls, so be kind to yourself, remember good enough parenting is good enough.

But most importantly, remember there is help out there. There is always someone to reach out to for support for your child, yourself, other family members or friends who may need a little support.

*"Start where you are. Use what you have. Do what you can."*
*- Arthur Ashe* [35]

# Chapter 12

# Connect and Play to Thrive: You've Got This!

*"There are only two lasting bequests we can hope to give our children. One of these is roots, the other, wings."*
*– Johann Wolfgang von Goethe*

As you know, I became a teacher before I became a parent. I stepped into the parenting journey with thousands and thousands of hours of experience, an abundance of theoretical knowledge and what can only be described as some ill placed confidence! But what I learned when I became a parent was that it doesn't matter who you are or what knowledge you possess. When you step into the arena of parenting, the key ingredient is YOU. It doesn't matter to your child if you are educated, uneducated, young, old, beautiful, ugly, rich, or poor, you are their source of love, their 'person', the one they need more than anything else.

You only have to watch the interaction between a baby and their mum and dad, to know this is true. A baby's search for eye contact, the serve and return of cooing and making little noises, to connect and bond all demonstrate the need for connection and a sense of feeling safe. I can guarantee you the little one couldn't care less if their 'person' owns the latest communication device or drives a luxury car. What matters most to them is that their mum, dad or carer shows up for them every single time.

Over the years as our two children grew, and we walked (sometimes crawled lol) along the journey of life together, it became obvious and apparent that they knew their Mum and Dad had their back (they felt safe, seen and secure), no matter how tricky or challenging a situation may have been. The reason that I can confidently say that is because they have both articulated it, at some point along the way. I don't share this for any other reason, but to say that as parents, all we did was show up. Sometimes they were not our finest moments, but other times we nailed it.

Our kids still talk about when they were younger how annoyed they used to be that their dad and I would insist on them being home by a certain time, whilst a few of their mates could play in the street well after dark. We had the boundaries in place and they knew we would hold the line. In fact, they tell us the boundaries came in handy sometimes when they didn't want to do something but felt the pressure to. They would blame their dad and I, which effectively gave them an out and enabled them to save face with their mates. Gotta love kids hey!

## *Defining Moments*

While we were knee deep in parenting our own kids, I was also heavily invested in my teaching career, with the sole aim of making a difference to the lives of kids. I remember the exact moment I decided I wanted to be a teacher; I was eight years old, sitting at the feet of my year 2 teacher and she was reading aloud to us. She was so caring, and kind and I remember thinking I wanted to be just like her and that was it. I never deviated from achieving my goal to teach, defining moment number one!

And just as a side note, to this day, one of my most favourite things to do is to read aloud, whether it is to Hudson or kids in the classroom, because it brings joy, a shared connection and a sense of belonging, because we are doing something that is joyful and in a moment of time, a connection point.

Which brings me to the next defining moment in my life and career, which coincidentally has to do with books. You may remember a defining moment from chapter one, a conversation with my daughter, which led to me writing this book. This book offers a way of sharing some information and connecting with others through words that may help parents to understand a little about what their child needs from them beyond a bottle, a bath, or bed. And hopefully, it also reassures readers that compassion for oneself and kids is paramount and can be the very thing that can protect us when things get a bit wobbly.

Defining moment number three has been an accumulation of things from my work supporting children and young people with complex and challenging behaviour. A big part of the work is understanding what is happening for a child or young person, because as you may recall, behaviour is communication, so as a team we are often asking ourselves that very question, what is trying to be communicated here, what need is not being met?

Once we understand the behaviour, through conversation with the child when they are regulated and calm, the escalation can be attributed to some or all of these things: not feeling safe, secure, connected or feeling like they belong. And when the dysregulated behaviour is explored some more, interestingly, often the one thing that arises in most cases is the experiences in very early childhood, for that child or young person. Maybe they have experienced a parent that didn't always show up for them or showed up spasmodically, or there were unfortunate events that led to trauma or prolonged stress.

This got me to thinking, we can't undo the past, but we can support and nurture the future for our kids and it can be as simple as connecting and playing, so our children and the children of others can thrive. My passion is about raising awareness and encouraging people to slow down and live in the moment a little more and release the pressure of trying to do everything and be perfect at it.

I'm sure you've all heard the quote or a version of it; *"it's not about the destination, it's about the journey"*. It's such a commonly used phrase, but I often wonder how many of us, including me, actually embody that? There is ample opportunity throughout our daily lives to practice it and just being aware, we can be a little more in the moment and create those lasting relationships and connections not just with our kids, but also others. I also acknowledge it is easier said than done sometimes, especially in the fast-paced world we live in. But there are glimmers every day. We just need to notice them.

We've talked about the how critical play is, but just to reiterate, connecting through play is something we all have at our disposal every moment of the day and can look different for everyone. If we think of it as a vehicle to build and strengthen our relationship with our kids then it opens up a world for them to flourish and thrive.

If you take a moment to reflect on your childhood, without judgment, and think about your favourite memories, I can hazard a guess that amongst those favourite memories are times of fun with significant people, such as parents, siblings, and grandparents.

One of my fondest memories is being with my siblings in a trailer being towed down a dirt road with my grandfather at the wheel of the car. We were laughing so hard, and my grandfather was trying to find every bump in the road to make us laugh even harder! We still talk about it to this very day! Definitely not the safest of activities, and no, you wouldn't do it nowadays, but hey no judgment, it was just the way it was back in the day.

My Pop wasn't your average sort of Pop, but he loved having fun with us and we all knew he loved us. We had a lovely connection with him and full faith he would keep us safe, which is pretty funny especially given that particular activity, but we were oblivious to any danger, cause we knew he had our backs.

Another of my fondest memories is with my kids, when I decided to change up their dinner one night, from a very sensible plate filled with vegetables and a little protein, to a plate that looked entirely different from other nights. It had yoghurt, dried fruit, and a range of other healthy options (making me feel as though I was still feeding my kids well lol), but to the kids it was very different, and it looked fun. I remember their little faces beaming and thinking how special it was that their dinner was out of the ordinary. I also remember not having one moan or groan about having to eat broccoli or beans, and they cleaned their plates. This is also one of those memories that's raised every so often by our kids and they laugh, saying how much they loved it. At the time it was a small thing, little did I know it would be a big thing, that built connection and the relationship with our kids.

When I reflect on those memories, I also noticed that each of them had common qualities; moments with significant people, a sensory aspect to them, such as movement or tasting food, as well as some predictability. All aspects we have talked about along our journey in this book, that help to build a sense of safety, a sense of belonging and connection.

I have a hunch some of your fondest memories will include those qualities as well, rather than a memory of a receiving 'thing', such as a new bike. Unless, of course that bike means fond memories of your Nanna teaching you how to ride it down the road, with her running beside, saying, "you are doing it, you are doing it!", as was the case for me.

I think Mona Delahooke, PhD (2022), encapsulates it beautifully when she says:

> *"To help our children flourish, we can plan less, relax more and recognise that we don't need to work so hard at parenting."* [36]

## Connect and Play to Thrive: You've Got This!

I love this quote as it sums up all that we need to be aware of and if we try each day to practice it, then we are a long way down the track to knowing how to be with our kids, and tuning into what they may need from us at different times.

Which leads me to one last 'lesson' or practice for this book, as I've said, once a teacher, always a teacher!

Something you may not know about teachers is that we love a checklist. It's a weird thing but one that is almost synonymous with being a teacher. So, I could not think of a better way to close out this book than with a checklist. It is not a checklist of must dos or the formula to perfect parenting, but a checklist that prompts thinking and is an easy reference point if times are tough and you need to take a moment to nurture your wellbeing as well as your child's. I hope you find it helpful and useful at a time of need.

Suggestion of things to consider to build resilience, increase a sense of connection and belonging and build a solid foundation for your child's emotional development:

- ☐ Place Relationships on Top of the List - spend quality time with your kids, really listen to what's on their minds, and create a trusting and understanding atmosphere. It's about *being with your child*.

- ☐ Go with the Flow - be open, present and flexible, letting your kids' interests and curiosity lead the way. Stay in the moment and be flexible, and you'll build stronger and more genuine connections with them that you'll both remember.

☐ Discover Daily Moments of Connection - finding those everyday moments to connect with your kids is all about looking for chances to engage with them on a personal level. It could be having a chat about their day, playing together, or just sharing a good laugh or a hug. These little, but special moments can make your bond stronger and create lasting memories for both you and your kids.

☐ Infuse Some Safe and Spontaneous Fun - adding a dose of safe and unplanned fun into the mix with your kids brings extra joy and excitement to your daily routine. Whether it's surprising them with a game, breaking into a spontaneous dance session, or working on a creative project together, these moments of laughter and play lead to an enhanced sense of belonging and security.

☐ Enhance the Comfort Factor - boosting the comfort level between kids and parents means making a cozy and open atmosphere where children can freely talk about their feelings. It's all about being good listeners, understanding their worries, and keeping the lines of communication wide open. This helps parents and kids build trust and a close bond, so kids know their mum or dad have their back.

Well, I guess we are ending where we began: is this parenting gig a job or a journey? I hope this book has given you some insight into the answer to that question. It really is a journey, one filled with sunshine, joy, fears and challenges! Additionally, I hope it has shed some light on the critical role we as parents play in our children's lives. Not just as providers of food, a warm bath and a nice comfy bed, but as nurturers and protectors of our children's emotional development and sense of self.

The relationship between us as parents and our kids is fundamental to their sense of feeling safe, calm, and secure. Our relationship is the framework for knowing what our kids need from us, but also the basis for helping them manage all that life will present them with along the way. The relationship provides a secure base for them to navigate the challenges, share the joys and support them in developing a strong sense of self, so that they can eventually succeed in their own unique way.

Parenting is a blessing and I hope this book has shown that the role of good enough parenting is not just significant, but essential in the journey of raising happy and emotionally connected kids. It reminds us that perfection is not the goal; rather, it is the genuine love, support, and effort we offer that truly matters.

By showing kindness to both yourself and your kids, being a 'good enough' parent sets a solid foundation and will give your kids the confidence to venture on their own unique journeys towards a fulfilling and meaningful life.

I wish you many moments of warmth, connection and sheer joy with your children and a lifetime of cherished memories and wellbeing as I leave you with this beautiful quote:

> *"They will not look back on their childhood and remember how clean the house was or how much TV they watched. They are going to remember how they felt when you hugged them, and the bedtime books you read them. They will remember the silly Mum who danced with them and the mum who explored with them. They will remember the moments they spent with you."* – Nadia Tayob [37]

# Acknowledgments

As I reflect upon the completion of my book, "Beyond, Bottles, Baths, and Bed: The Complete Guide to Raising Happy Emotionally Connected Kids," it's impossible to overstate the debt of gratitude I owe to the numerous individuals who have made this journey possible. Writing a book is not a solitary pursuit, and it's with heartfelt appreciation that I acknowledge those who have contributed to this endeavour in many ways.

First and foremost, I want to express my deep appreciation to my husband, Gary. Your unwavering support, patience, and belief in me has been nothing short of extraordinary. Your continued encouragement during moments of doubt propelled me forward.

To my children, Jake and Samara, you both inspire me daily. As I wrote about nurturing emotionally connected kids, I saw the living embodiment of those principles in both of you. Thank you for your support and for providing endless love and inspiration. I hope that this book serves as a reminder of the values we hold dear as a family.

To my parents, Mum and Dad, your love, guidance, and the values you instilled in me have provided the foundation for this work. I am grateful for your unwavering belief in me and your unending support. Your example of strong family connections served as the driving force behind my writing.

My sister, Sue, and my brother, Peter, you have played a significant role in shaping who I am today. You've been my most loyal supporters from the very beginning and your constant support, encouragement and laughs are something I cherish.

To my son in-law, Hayden, and daughter in-law, Ishka, thank you for your support and positivity, you are both amazing additions to our family. You embody the values we all hold dear as family and I have no doubt Hudson, his future siblings and cousins will flourish through your parenting.

My colleagues and fellow educators, with whom I have shared the joys and challenges of my teaching career, deserve special mention. Our shared experiences, discussions, and insights have indelibly shaped the content of this book. I'm grateful for the collaborative spirit that infused our work together.

Lastly, to the readers, supporters, and well-wishers who have embraced "Beyond, Bottles, Baths, and Bed," your interest in my work gives it purpose and meaning. My hope is that this book serves as a guiding light in your journey of raising happy and emotionally connected children.

In closing, I am incredibly grateful to each and every one of you for being a part of this journey. "Beyond, Bottles, Baths, and Bed" is a testament to the power of collaboration, encouragement, and the unwavering support of a loving community. Together, we can shape a brighter future for the next generation of emotionally connected children.

With deepest gratitude,
Cherie

# About the Author

Cherie King is first and foremost a very proud mother of two amazing adult children who continue to bring joy to her life every day. She recently became a grandmother for the first time and is delighting in the opportunity to do it all again, but this time with a little more wisdom and way more fun!

A qualified teacher who holds a Bachelor of Education with 30 + years of teaching experience, Cherie has worked with in excess of 1000 children and young people. She has held numerous positions throughout the course of her career including as the principal of three primary schools in New South Wales, Australia.

Over the years, Cherie has significantly enhanced and refined her knowledge and skills through comprehensive professional growth. This growth encompasses areas such as trauma-informed practice, coregulation, ADHD and Autism. She holds a high level of expertise in supporting families and schools with children who experience dysregulation or stress reactions in various environments.

Cherie is passionate about helping parents, in fact all adults, understand how the body informs the brain and acknowledging as humans we have a hardwired need for connection and belonging. Being aware of the need is vital for overall well-being as it impacts mental health, emotional regulation, resilience, physical health, and our ability to form meaningful relationships.

Sharing her years of knowledge and expertise in a way that is simple and easy to follow, Cherie gives parents the confidence to flip their thinking to viewing parenting as a journey, not a job. She acknowledges the journey is hard, crazy hard, but through compassion for kids and themselves, parents can build deep connections and strong relationships that last a lifetime and have profound positive impacts on wellbeing, self-identity and belonging.

Currently, she resides on the far north coast of New South Wales with her husband. In her leisure time, Cherie enjoys spending quality moments with her adult children, their partners, and her grandson. Additionally, she takes pleasure in traveling, savouring good food, and cherishing time with family and friends.

# References

1 Brown, B. (2012). *Daring Greatly: How the Courage to Be Vulnerable Transforms the Way We Live, Love, Parent, and Lead.* London: Penguin Books Ltd. pg. 232 & 233

2 Brotherson, Sean. *FS-609 APRIL 2005 BRIGHT BEGINNINGS #4.* 2005.

3 Siegel, D.J. and Bryson, T.P. (2011a). *The Whole-Brain Child: 12 Revolutionary Strategies to Nurture Your child's Developing Mind.* New York: Bantam Books. pg. 3

4 Siegel, D.J. and Bryson, T.P. (2011b). *The Whole-Brain Child: 12 Revolutionary Strategies to Nurture Your child's Developing Mind.* New York: Bantam Books. pg. 4

5 Siegel, D.J. and Bryson, T.P. (2011b). *The Whole-Brain Child: 12 Revolutionary Strategies to Nurture Your child's Developing Mind.* New York: Bantam Books. pg.12 & 13

6 Siegel, D.J. and Bryson, T.P. (2021a). *POWER OF SHOWING UP: how parental presence shapes who our kids become and how their brains get wired.* New York: Ballantine. Pg.5

7 Siegel, D.J. and Bryson, T.P. (2021b). *POWER OF SHOWING UP: how parental presence shapes who our kids become and how their brains get wired.* New York: Ballantine. pg. 4

8 Siegel, D.J. and Bryson, T.P. (2021c). *POWER OF SHOWING UP: how parental presence shapes who our kids become and how their brains get wired.* New York: Ballantine. pg. 5

9 Siegel, D.J. and Bryson, T.P. (2021c). *POWER OF SHOWING UP: how parental presence shapes who our kids become and how their brains get wired.* New York: Ballantine. pg. 5

9Articles·, F.N. (2021). *How Neurons That Wire Together Fire Together.* [online] Neuroscience News.

10 Hoffman, K. (2017). *Raising a secure child: how circle of security parenting can help you nurture your child's attachment, emotional resilience, and freedom to explore.* New York: Guilford Press.

11 Siegel, D.J. and Bryson, T.P. (2021d). *POWER OF SHOWING UP: how parental presence shapes who our kids become and how their brains get wired.* New York: Ballantine. Pg.62

12 Delahooke, M. (2022a). Brain-Body Parenting. HarperCollins.

13 Delahooke, M. (2022a). Brain-Body Parenting. HarperCollins.

14 Columbus Metropolitan Club (2014). *Bruce Perry, Early Childhood Brain Development. YouTube.* Available at: https://www.youtube.com/watch?v=DXdBFFph2QQ.

## References

15 Delahooke, M. (2022a). Brain-Body Parenting. HarperCollins.

16 Rosanbalm, K. (2017). *Promoting Self-Regulation in the First Five Years: A Practice Brief.* [online] Available at: https://fpg.unc.edu/sites/fpg.unc.edu/files/resources/reports-and-policy-briefs/PromotingSelf-RegulationIntheFirstFiveYears.pdf.

17 Delahooke, M. (2022b). *Brain-Body Parenting.* HarperCollins. Pg.100

1 Delahooke, M. (2022c). *Brain-Body Parenting.* HarperCollins. pg. 110

18 Oxfordlearnersdictionaries.com. (2023). *emotional-intelligence noun - Definition, pictures, pronunciation and usage notes | Oxford Advanced Learner's Dictionary at OxfordLearnersDictionaries.com.*

19 Siegel, D.J. (2010). *Mindsight: the New Science of Personal Transformation.* New York: Bantam Books.

20 Delahooke, M. (2022d). *Brain-Body Parenting.* HarperCollins. pg.123

21 Parenting Research Centre. (n.d.). *Parenting Today in Victoria.* [online] Available at: https://www.parentingrc.org.au/publications/parenting-today-in-victoria/

22 "Just Say No to Judgment: How Judging Parents Actually Leads to Worse, Not Better, Outcomes for Kids." *ZERO to THREE,* www.zerotothree.org/resource/just-say-no-to-judgment-how-judging-parents-actually-leads-to-worse-not-better-outcomes-for-kids/. (22)

23 Delahooke, M. (2022e). *Brain-Body Parenting*. HarperCollins. pg.141 & 142

24 Delahooke, M. (2022f). Brain-Body Parenting. HarperCollins. pg.142

25 Delahooke, M. (2022g). Brain-Body Parenting. HarperCollins. pg.153

26 www.mja.com.au. (n.d.). *Volume 218, Issue 6 Supplement | The Medical Journal of Australia*. [online] Available at: https://www.mja.com.au/journal/2023/218/6/supplement.

27 Goodall, E. (2016). *Ready to learn Interoception kit.* [online] Available at: https://www.education.sa.gov.au/docs/support-and-inclusion/engagement-and-wellbeing/ready-to-learn-interoception-kit.pdf. (26) Preface page

28 Delahooke, M. (2022h). *Brain-Body Parenting*. HarperCollins. pg.162

29 Wright, M. (2021). *How every child can thrive by five.* [online] www.ted.com. Available at: https://www.ted.com/talks/molly_wright_how_every_child_can_thrive_by_five.

30 Yogman, M., Garner, A., Hutchinson, J., Hirsh-Pasek, K. and Golinkoff, R.M. (2018). The power of play: A pediatric role in enhancing development in young children. *Pediatrics*, [online] 142(3). doi:https://doi.org/10.1542/peds.2018-2058.

31 www.youtube.com. (n.d.). *To a child love is spelled TIME | ZIG ZIGLAR*. [online] Available at: https://www.youtube.com/

## References

watch?app=desktop&v=eKso4KdV_OI [Accessed 22 Oct. 2023]. (31)

32 Delahooke, M. (2022i). *Brain-Body Parenting*. HarperCollins. (31) pg. 256-257

34 Jamison, K.R. and Dunne, B. (2008). *Exuberance: The Passion For Life*. New York: Books on Tape.

35 Anon, (2022). *'Start Where You Are. Use What You Have. Do What You Can.' – Arthur Ashe - University of Pacific*. [online] Available at: https://pacific.edu.ni/start-where-you-are-use-what-you-have-do-what-you-can-arthur-ashe/#:~:text=Where%20You%20Are.-.

36 Delahooke, M. (2022j). *Brain-Body Parenting*. HarperCollins. pg.286

37 T, N. (2020). *40 Heartwarming Quotes About Loving Children*. [online] Fun with Mama. Available at: https://www.funwithmama.com/beautiful-quotes-about-loving-children/ [Accessed 23 Oct. 2023].

# Bibliography

Brown, Brené. *Daring Greatly: How the Courage to Be Vulnerable Transforms the Way We Live, Love, Parent, and Lead.* New York, Ny, Gotham Books, 2012.

Brown, Stuart L, and Christopher C Vaughan. *Play: How It Shapes the Brain, Opens the Imagination, and Invigorates the Soul.* New York, Avery, 2009.

Delahooke, Mona. *Beyond Behaviours: Using Brain Science and Compassion to Understand and Solve Children's Behavioural Challenges.* London, John Murray, 2019.

---. *Brain-Body Parenting.* HarperCollins, 15 Mar. 2022.

Dix, Paul. *AFTER the ADULTS CHANGE: Achievable Behaviour Nirvana.* S.L., Independent Thinking Pr, 2021. *When the Adults Change, Everything Changes: Seismic Shifts in School Behaviour.* Bancyfelin, Independent Thinking Press, 2017.

Garland, Teresa. *Self-Regulation Interventions and Strategies: Keeping the Body, Mind and Emotions on Task in Children with Autism, ADHD or Sensory Disorders.* Eau Claire, Wisconsin, Pesi Publishing & Media, 2014.

Greene, Ross W. *Explosive Child: A New Approach for Understanding and Parenting Easily Frustrated, Chronically... Inflexible Children.* S.L., Harpercollins, 2021.

Hoffman, Kent. *Raising a Secure Child: How Circle of Security Parenting Can Help You Nurture Your Child's Attachment, Emotional Resilience, and Freedom to Explore.* New York, Guilford Press, 2017.

Jamison, Kay R. *Exuberance: The Passion for Life.* New York, Vintage Books, 2005.

Maslow, A. H. *A Theory of Human Motivation.* 1943. Lanham, Start Publishing LLC, 2019.

MeAIMH. "Polyvagel Theory." *Maine Association for Infant Mental Health*, 10 Mar. 2022, www.infantmentalhealth.org/polyvagel-theory.

News, Neuroscience. "How Neurons That Wire Together Fire Together." *Neuroscience News*, 23 Dec. 2021, neurosciencenews.com/wire-fire-neurons-19835/. Accessed 24 Oct. 2023.

Olrick, Amy Elizabeth, and Jeffrey. *The 6 Needs of Every Child.* Zondervan, 9 June 2020.

Owen, J B. *Enjoying Parenting.* Jbo Global, 1 Nov. 2020.

Page Rendering Error | OECD ILibrary. *Www.oecd-Ilibrary.org*, www.oecd-ilibrary.org/sites/c9881f36-en/index.html?itemId=/content/component/c9881f36-en. Accessed 24 Oct. 2023.

*Bibliography*

Parenting Today in Victoria. *Parenting Research Centre*, www.parentingrc.org.au/publications/parenting-today-in-victoria/.

PORGES, S. W. "The Polyvagal Theory: New Insights into Adaptive Reactions of the Autonomic Nervous System." *Cleveland Clinic Journal of Medicine*, vol. 76, no. Suppl_2, 2009, pp. S86–S90, www.ncbi.nlm.nih.gov/pmc/articles/PMC3108032/, https://doi.org/10.3949/ccjm.76.s2.17.

*Ready to Learn Interoception Kit.* 2019.

Rosanbalm, KD. *Promoting Self-Regulation in the First Five Years: A Practice Brief.* 2017.

Schow. "Just Say No to Judgment: How Judging Parents Actually Leads to Worse, Not Better, Outcomes for Kids." *ZERO to THREE*, www.zerotothree.org/resource/just-say-no-to-judgment-how-judging-parents-actually-leads-to-worse-not-better-outcomes-for-kids/.

Shanker, Stuart. *Reframed: Self-Reg for a Just Society.* Toronto; Buffalo ; London, University Of Toronto Press, 2020.

Siegel, Daniel J, and Tina Payne Bryson. *POWER of SHOWING up: How Parental Presence Shapes Who Our Kids Become and How Their Brains Get Wired.* New York, Ballantine, 2021.

*The Whole-Brain Child : 12 Revolutionary Strategies to Nurture Your Child's Developing Mind.* New York, Bantam Books, 2011.

Van de Veer, Rene. "(PDF) Vygotsky's Theory." *ResearchGate*, 2020, www.researchgate.net/publication/339136533_Vygotsky.

"Volume 218, Issue 6 Supplement | the Medical Journal of Australia." *Www.mja.com.au*, www.mja.com.au/journal/2023/218/6/supplement.

Winfrey, Oprah, and Dr Bruce Perry. *What Happened to You?* Boxtree, 27 Apr. 2021.

Yogman, Michael, et al. "The Power of Play: A Pediatric Role in Enhancing Development in Young Children." *Pediatrics*, vol. 142, no. 3, 20 Aug. 2018, publications.aap.org/pediatrics/article/142/3/e20182058/38649/The-Power-of-Play-A-Pediatric-Role-in-Enhancing?autologincheck=redirected, https://doi.org/10.1542/peds.2018-2058.

*Nifplay.org*, 2023, www.nifplay.org/. Accessed 24 Oct. 2023.

# Kick Start or Supercharge Your Connection Journey. Free 30 Day Connection Challenge.

Connect Play Thrive

- 30 Day free challenge for building lasting memories
- Sign up today to start having fun & connecting immediately
- Month filled with laughter, joy, and unforgettable bonding experiences
- Fun & easy activity delivered daily to your inbox for 30 days
- Embrace the magic of connection and play
- Positive impact on family dynamic
- Embark on a journey of discovery and joy with your kids

**30-DAY FREE CONNECTION CHALLENGE**

To sign up for the challenge email:
support@connectplaythrive.com

# SPECIAL OFFER

**40% OFF**
The cost of a one hour 1 to 1 session for new clients

## 1 TO 1 SUPPORT

Parenting can be a wild ride, and I am here to make sure you've got a seasoned co-pilot. Introducing my exclusive 1-to-1 support sessions—your personal lifeline in the parenting adventure! Whether you're navigating the terrible twos, managing meltdowns or just in need of a friendly ear, I am ready to customise strategies that work for your unique family dynamic.

It's not about one-size-fits-all solutions; it's about creating a support system tailored just for you. Say goodbye to the guesswork and hello to personalised, practical advice that transforms challenges into victories.

Enjoy an exclusive 40% off a one hour session as a heartfelt thank you for choosing to work with me. It's my way of saying hello and inviting you to experience the best at a fraction of the cost. Dive into this special introductory offer and access the tools and knowledge to connect, understand and supercharge your relationship with your child.

Book your 1-to-1 session today and let's make parenting a journey filled with confidence, clarity, and a whole lot of joy!

*Enjoy an exclusive 40% off the cost of a one hour 1 to 1 support session for new clients.*

Contact: support@connectplaythrive.com

www.connectplaythrive.com

# Cherie King

### Transformational Speaker, Educator & Author

Cherie is passionate about helping parents, carers, and educators understand how the body informs the brain and acknowledging as humans we have a hardwired need for connection and belonging. Being aware of the need is vital for overall well-being as it impacts mental health, emotional regulation, resilience, physical health, and our ability to form meaningful relationships.

A passionate and down to earth speaker, Cherie connects immediately with her audience and leaves them feeling empowered and confident to take on the ever-changing adventure that is parenting or working with kids.

## SIGNATURE TOPICS

- ✓ Connection is the Key
- ✓ The Superpower of Play to Build Connection
- ✓ Unlocking the Toddler Code
- ✓ The Magic of "Showing Up"
- ✓ Happiness Unleashed: The Power of Emotional Intelligence

## TO ENQUIRE ABOUT BOOKING CHERIE FOR YOUR NEXT EVENT:

E: cherie@connectplaythrive.com

Ph: 0487579144

www.connectplaythrive.com

f Connect Play Thrive   Connect Play Thrive   connectplaythrive

# Notes

www.ingramcontent.com/pod-product-compliance
Lightning Source LLC
Chambersburg PA
CBHW041140110526
44590CB00027B/4081